Get the eBook FREE!
(PDF, ePub, Kindle, and liveBook all included)

We believe that once you buy a book from us, you should be able to read it in any format we have available. To get electronic versions of this book at no additional cost to you, purchase and then register this book at the Manning website.

Go to https://www.manning.com/freebook and follow the instructions to complete your pBook registration.

That's it!
Thanks from Manning!

AWS for Non-Engineers

AWS for Non-Engineers

HIROKO NISHIMURA

MANNING
SHELTER ISLAND

Manning Publications Co.
20 Baldwin Road
PO Box 761
Shelter Island, NY 11964

Development editor: Bobbie Jennings
Review editor: Aleksandar Dragosavljević
Production editor: Keri Hales
Copy editor: Alisa Larson
Proofreader: Jason Everett
Typesetter: Gordan Salinovic
Cover designer: Marija Tudor

ISBN 9781633439948
Printed in the United States of America

This book is dedicated to Baby C, who cheered—er—kicked me on throughout the last half of the manuscript. I put the last edits to this manuscript in my third trimester, and by the time I hold a copy of this book in my hands, I anticipate I would have spent a few sleepless months already.

Baby C, Mommy hasn't met you yet, but has loved you since the moment she found out you were joining the family.

brief contents

contents

preface

My transition into the world of tech was an accidental one. I graduated from university in 2014 with a bachelor's degree and master's degree in special education but with my desire to teach in the classroom snuffed out. Simultaneously overqualified (because of my master's degree) and underqualified (because I had no work experience, especially in anything that didn't have to do with teaching kids), I made my way to New York City and began looking for a job. It took half a year and hundreds of résumés, but I managed to land a job as an IT helpdesk engineer (I applied to be their in-house recruiter). While I had never envisioned a career in tech for myself, I suddenly found myself surrounded by computers, servers, printers, and frantic phone calls from coworkers that all required my attention.

A few years later, I began my exploration into Amazon Web Services and was immediately stuck. I had promised my manager at the time that I was going to take the AWS Certified Cloud Practitioner exam, but two weeks prior to the exam date I was no closer to understanding even *what* AWS was than I was before I began studying.

I realized that even though the exam was marketed for those who may have very little experience with IT or AWS, the exam preparation courses had not yet caught up with this new demographic and were mostly reusing content for the more technical certification exams, like the AWS Solutions Architect Associates exam. While there are huge overlaps in content, the way the information was presented needed to be modified substantially to cater to the new demographic of people who not only are "cloud newbies," but also "IT newbies" because the AWS Certified Cloud Practitioner exam's target demographic doesn't necessarily have legacy IT infrastructure background (or vocabulary).

After a lot of back and forth with myself on how to best prepare for the certification exam, I created awsnewbies.com as my own exam study guide. I used it myself to pass the certification exam and decided to leave it up for a year, hoping it may help one or two other people.

Things escalated very quickly after that. Within a few months, I had a contract with LinkedIn Learning to create online video courses with them to introduce Amazon Web Services to people with no technical backgrounds. "Introduction to AWS for Non-Engineers" (introtoaws.com) was a huge hit, and the courses were recently translated into Spanish and Portuguese!

There was a definite pain point in people wanting to learn about cloud computing and Amazon Web Services, but not knowing where to find beginner-friendly, jargon-free resources to get started. Through my work creating beginner-friendly content and teaching hundreds of thousands of people who were eager to learn, I had the honor of being named an AWS Community Hero in 2020.

When I received an email from Manning wondering if I'd be interested in writing an introductory AWS book, I decided that a reference book would supplement my other content very well in helping people break into cloud computing and Amazon Web Services. People have all sorts of learning styles, and some people learn better visually or with audio and others, by reading. This book, along with video courses and a website, would help cater to all those types of learners!

acknowledgments

I'd like to thank my mother, without whom I wouldn't be here (literally), who nursed me back to health after my brain surgery. She allowed me to explore the world to find out what I can "still do" despite my new brain injury, even though it was probably one of the scariest things she could do as a mother.

I'd also like to thank my husband, who has been a relentless cheerleader from the beginning of my out-of-the-box career maneuvers, believing there was something there even when I wasn't convinced.

There are countless people I owe for giving me a spotlight or a hand to pull me up a step as I began exploring the world of AWS and helping other AWS newbies learn about the cloud—many of whom I have yet to even meet in person. There are too many to name, but I hope I have been able to pay their kindness forward with the work I have been doing over the past few years.

At Manning, my amazing editor, Bobbie Jennings, flew in like a superhero and made the writing and editing process so much easier for me. I was able to bust out the last half of the book in just a few short months with her support, and I'm super grateful for her involvement with this—at times, rather tedious—process. I'd also like to thank the production staff for their hard work in creating this book.

Finally, thanks to all the reviewers: Amogh Raghunath, Bhagvan Kommadi, Christian Sutton, Dave Alonso, Dinesh Reddy Chittibala, Eric Thomas Anderson, Frankie Thomas-Hockey, Ganesh Swaminathan, Hridyesh Singh Bisht, Jereme Allen, Jeremy

Chen, Jessica van der Berg, Juan Luis Barreda, Leonardo Anastasia, Mariana Andelman, Oliver Korten, Rajiv Moghe, Rodrigo Pinheiro de Almeida, Shalini Menezes, Shweta Joshi, Ulrich Gauger, Vanessa Correia, and Zachery Beyel. Your suggestions helped make this a better book.

about this book

AWS for Non-Engineers focuses on introducing cloud computing and Amazon Web Services with beginner-friendly language and concepts. While the title has "Non-Engineers" in it, it is a shorthand for "You don't need to come in with any technical background" and doesn't mean this book can't help engineers and IT professionals with years, or decades, of IT experience. It is a reference book and also serves as an exam preparation book for the AWS Certified Cloud Practitioner exam.

Who should read this book

AWS for Non-Engineers is a no-frills book with minimal jargon that aims to introduce cloud computing and Amazon Web Services to those with and without technical backgrounds. This book is geared toward both people looking to transition into tech from an unrelated field and those who have experience in working in tech but would like a generalized introduction to AWS.

You may be a sales person working at a Software as a Service company, a finance person working in a tech startup, or a lawyer working at a company looking into utilizing cloud computing for its IT solution. Or you may be a developer or IT engineer looking to dip your toes into cloud computing and want a beginner-friendly introduction. Regardless of your technical background, if you are looking to take the AWS Certified Cloud Practitioner exam, this book is definitely for you!

How this book is organized: A road map

This book has two major focuses: introducing you to the AWS Cloud and helping you to prepare for the AWS Certified Cloud Practitioner exam.

The first six chapters of the book introduce you to Amazon Web Services (AWS Cloud), cloud computing, and the AWS Certified Cloud Practitioner exam. It also dives into cloud concepts, AWS's global infrastructure, core AWS services, security and compliance topics in AWS (including security services), and billing and pricing concepts:

- Chapter 1 introduces cloud computing, its value proposition, and Amazon Web Services. It will also briefly introduce the AWS Certified Cloud Practitioner exam for those interested.
- Chapter 2 discusses cloud concepts, such as the advantages of cloud computing, types of cloud computing models and deployments, and design principles in cloud computing.
- Chapter 3 describes the global AWS infrastructure and how you can deploy and operate in AWS.
- Chapter 4 introduces core AWS services like compute services, storage services, database services, networking and content delivery services, and management tools.
- Chapter 5 discusses security and compliance concepts and core AWS security services.
- Chapter 6 shares billing and pricing concepts, tools to help understand your AWS costs, and the AWS support plans.
- Chapter 7 re-introduces the AWS Certified Cloud Practitioner exam and goes deep into deconstructing the logistics and the content. The chapter includes study aids to help with the exam preparation. This chapter prepares you to take the AWS Certified Cloud Practitioner exam by bringing together what you learned throughout the previous six chapters.

The book is meant to be read from beginning to end, unless you have no intention of taking the AWS Certified Cloud Practitioner exam, in which case, you don't need to read chapter 7 since it goes in-depth by bringing together all the concepts and services and tying them together with the exam content. However, I hope that while reading the book, you may realize that you might be up to sitting for the exam. If that's the case, I wish you the best of luck!

The contents for four exam domains for AWS Certified Cloud Practitioner Exam are introduced in the book as follows:

- *Domain 1, Cloud Concepts*—Chapter 2
- *Domain 2, Security and Compliance*—Chapter 5
- *Domain 3, Technology*—Chapter 3 and chapter 4
- *Domain 4, Billing and Pricing*—Chapter 6

liveBook discussion forum

Purchase of *AWS for Non-Engineers* includes free access to liveBook, Manning's online reading platform. Using liveBook's exclusive discussion features, you can attach comments to the book globally or to specific sections or paragraphs. It's a snap to make notes for yourself, ask and answer technical questions, and receive help from the author and other users. To access the forum, go to https://livebook.manning.com/book/aws-for-non-engineers/discussion. You can also learn more about Manning's forums and the rules of conduct at https://livebook.manning.com/discussion.

Manning's commitment to our readers is to provide a venue where a meaningful dialogue between individual readers and between readers and the author can take place. It is not a commitment to any specific amount of participation on the part of the author, whose contribution to the forum remains voluntary (and unpaid). We suggest you try asking the author some challenging questions lest her interest stray! The forum and the archives of previous discussions will be accessible from the publisher's website as long as the book is in print.

Other online resources

- If you are interested in learning about introductory AWS content taught in similar style as this book, catered toward people without background knowledge in tech, I have four video courses with LinkedIn Learning titled "Introduction to AWS for Non-Engineers" that are also available in Spanish and Portuguese at www.introtoaws.com. These courses will collectively help you prepare for the AWS Certified Cloud Practitioner exam as well.
- freeCodeCamp offers a free, comprehensive, 12-hour AWS Certified Cloud Practitioner exam preparation course on YouTube taught by Andrew Brown of ExamPro: http://mng.bz/YKV7.
- Amazon Web Services has official exam preparation materials for the AWS Certified Cloud Practitioner exam, including free video courses and official sample questions at http://mng.bz/BZxw.

about the author

 **HIROKO NISHIMURA** is a special education teacher, turned helpdesk engineer, turned systems administrator, turned technical instructor and writer. She created awsnewbies.com in 2018 to study for her AWS Certified Cloud Practitioner exam, focusing on breaking down technical jargon and concepts for laypeople. Hiroko published "Introduction to AWS for Non-Engineers" (www.introtoaws.com) courses with LinkedIn Learning in 2019 to help people from nontraditional technical backgrounds learn about AWS. These courses also prepare them for taking the AWS Certified Cloud Practitioner exam. In 2020, Hiroko became an AWS Community Hero for her work in making AWS more accessible to people who come from diverse backgrounds.

about the cover illustration

The figure on the cover of *AWS for Non-Engineers* is "Fille Tschouwache," or "Chuvash Girl," taken from a collection by Jacques Grasset de Saint-Sauveur, published in 1788. Each illustration is finely drawn and colored by hand.

In those days, it was easy to identify where people lived and what their trade or station in life was just by their dress. Manning celebrates the inventiveness and initiative of the computer business with book covers based on the rich diversity of regional culture centuries ago, brought back to life by pictures from collections such as this one.

Introduction to cloud computing and Amazon Web Services

1

This chapter covers

- Cloud computing and AWS
- Why people utilize cloud computing
- When to use AWS/cloud computing
- AWS Certified Cloud Practitioner exam

When beginning a dive into new technical concepts or fields, I often start out feeling as though I don't have the vocabulary, background knowledge, or mental models to make sense of the information being conveyed. After a while, I feel inclined to give up, resigned to the fact that it was probably all "too technical" for me anyway. This was the feeling I was yet again having as I tried to decipher what *cloud computing* and *Amazon Web Services* (AWS) are and why they were suddenly so ubiquitous in the IT world.

You may be an IT help-desk engineer looking to move into cloud administration or an IT manager considering moving from managing legacy IT infrastructure to the cloud and hoping to obtain a high-level understanding of AWS Cloud. Or, you may be a career-changer hoping to make a transition into IT, and the AWS Certified Cloud Practitioner exam may help get your foot in the door. Perhaps you are a sales associate at a tech company looking to get a better understanding of what cloud computing and AWS can offer for your potential clients. Or, you may be reading this book with a completely different set of backgrounds and reasons. Whatever the reason for picking up this book may be, welcome!

Ever since I created AWS Newbies (awsnewbies.com) to address my own needs to have AWS explained to me jargon-free, I have been creating resources and courses that have helped countless people around the world learn about AWS, all with their own unique backgrounds, which may or may not be technical. While there are countless great resources available for people to learn the intermediate- and advanced-level topics on AWS, I found that an *actually* beginner-friendly introduction was missing— one that assumes no prerequisite knowledge or technical background to begin learning about AWS. Over the past few years, it has been my pleasure to create and publish content that helps others realize that AWS isn't "just too technical" and that it's something anyone can definitely get more involved in.

In this first chapter, we discuss what cloud computing and AWS are, why people and companies use cloud computing over legacy IT infrastructure (or what we've been using for decades to take care of IT), and who should read this book. We then begin piecing together the ecosystem so you can get a better grasp of where all the different parts of cloud computing and AWS fit together in the grand scheme of things. Finally, we introduce the AWS Certified Cloud Practitioner exam, a foundational-level certification offered by AWS that will help you validate your knowledge of core cloud computing concepts and AWS services. While the goal to pass the exam is not a necessity for reading this book, the concepts you learn about translate very well in preparing for the exam.

Whether you're an IT professional diving into AWS for the first time or someone who has no traditional technical background, this book was written in the hopes that fewer people feel the sense of dread and confusion that I felt as they begin their investigation into the AWS Cloud and cloud computing. Let's get started!

1.1   *What is cloud computing?*

Even if you don't currently work in IT, you might be familiar with *file sharing*, where you can share with other computers the files, documents, and other electronic data that reside in your computer. Your work computer may have the ability to receive data from powerful computers called *servers*, where different users upload resources to share with their team or department. It might be where your marketing department saves branding and marketing graphics or your sales team saves contract templates.

Until recently, all of this data sharing happened *on premises* or within your company's office, such as in a server room, or in separate secured buildings known as *data centers*. With cloud computing, all of the physical IT infrastructure such as setting up server rooms, data centers, and purchasing and configuring physical servers is now taken care of by the cloud computing service providers such as AWS, Microsoft Azure, and Google Cloud Platform. We can now share resources and data with other computers using the internet instead of having to rely on our on-premises IT resources.

AWS (or AWS Cloud) is a cloud computing platform offered by the tech giant Amazon. To fully appreciate what AWS does, we need to back up and first define what cloud computing is. *Cloud computing*, according to AWS, is the "on-demand delivery of IT resources over the internet with pay-as-you-go pricing" (https://aws.amazon .com/what-is-cloud-computing/). In the most basic terms, cloud computing allows users to access IT resources using the internet instead of relying on whatever you have on hand locally (such as in your office). Instead of backing up your important files to your floppy disks (remember those?) or external hard drives, you can now back them up to the "cloud" by utilizing cloud computing services such as Box, Dropbox, and Google Drive.

On top of that, cloud computing services utilize pay-as-you-go pricing for their resources. Previously, when you wanted new IT equipment, you would make the purchase, paying for the whole piece of equipment up front. With pay-as-you-go pricing for cloud services, you only pay for however much IT resources you use, when you use them, as if you're paying your electricity or water bill.

IT infrastructure refers to all of the software and hardware components that make up a technical ecosystem. These can range from physical components such as data centers, servers, and computers to software components such as operating systems and specific pieces of software utilized in the company, such as Microsoft Office. In the context of this book, IT infrastructure can be physical, as in physical hardware, server rooms, or data centers, or virtual, as in accessed using the internet. You can think of it as everything you need to make sure your IT department is running smoothly.

Currently, I am writing this manuscript using Google Docs, a Google Cloud Platform service. I share manuscript drafts with my editor, and she, in turn, shares resources saved in cloud storage folders to help me edit and format my writing. When we are having meetings to discuss my book's directions, we hop on Skype for voice chats. From beginning to end, I am relying on cloud computing to plan and write this book. A decade or two before, the process of writing a book was very different. I may have still been writing on a computer, but I would probably save the file onto a floppy disk or USB drive and have in-person meetings with the editor. You, too, may be utilizing cloud computing platforms and services in many different parts of your work and personal life.

Globally, cloud computing has brought a huge change in the ways we interact with each other, work, and spend our days. Services such as Dropbox, Facebook, Google

Drive, and Slack that help us work and play are all fueled by cloud computing, and chances are, all of these major services are hosted on one of the few major cloud computing platforms. As of 2022, the largest share of cloud computing customers utilizes AWS.

1.2   Why cloud computing?

Let's imagine that you are looking to purchase a new laptop for yourself. You are a freelance graphic designer and need to run heavy (requires a lot of computing power to run efficiently) design and image editing software on it. You'll also be saving large files such as images, videos, and iterations of projects, which means you need a lot of storage. To meet these needs, you'll likely need a fairly high-specification computer so that you aren't spending 30 minutes trying to save a heavy (large file size) image file.

Buying a lot of storage and processing power gets expensive. But the computer's technical specifications aren't the only things you need to consider before you make your purchase. You go to client meetings and work in cafes a lot, so the computer needs to be portable, which means that its weight and size also become issues to consider. How quickly you need this new laptop is another consideration. Is your current computer broken, so you need a replacement as soon as possible, or can you wait a few weeks or even months to save a bit of money, potentially on a holiday sale? Also, do you go with an operating system that you have been using for years, or do you switch to a new one for pricing or user-experience reasons?

When purchasing new technical equipment like a computer, you often end up juggling technical specifications, size, speed of delivery, ease of use, and price. As a result, thanks to real-life limitations such as time, budget, and physical needs (you don't want to carry around a 15-pound desktop computer and monitor to client meetings), you often have to make compromises.

Scaled up hundreds- and thousands-fold, companies, large and small, encounter similar considerations, constraints, and compromises when evaluating purchases of new IT resources. What kind of equipment can we afford? How long will shipping take for this mission-critical server? How much space do we have in our office to create a server room to keep all of our servers and networking gear housed? Can we afford the labor, equipment, and renovation costs to have our own data center to keep our digital backups and servers in a safe location? How much will cooling the data center cost?

Cloud computing helps alleviate many, if not all, of these constraints and concerns with its on-demand delivery of IT resources such as computing power, storage, databases, and networking over the internet. Do you need a new server for your team's new web application development? It takes just minutes to configure and set up a virtual server, and it's ready to go! You will get a bill every month for the amount of computing resources you consumed while you used the server, which means you no longer have to worry about purchasing a server that wasn't just the right fit for your needs, potentially wasting a lot of money and time.

Outside of the corporate setting, cloud computing has revolutionized technology in our personal lives as well. Many services we take for granted these days, such as cloud-based email (Gmail, Yahoo! Mail), cloud storage (Dropbox, iCloud), streaming services (Netflix, Hulu), and social media (Twitter, Facebook), utilize cloud computing to provide us with quick, affordable, reliable, and on-demand services. Many of us rely on at least one cloud computing-based service every single day, whether it be using Google Maps to navigate to a Mexican restaurant, backing up photos from our phones to Google Photos, or asking Amazon Alexa for the weather forecast. Even your favorite vacuuming robot likely utilizes cloud computing to map out your house to clean more efficiently.

Gone are the days when we had to walk around with a USB thumb drive to move files from computer to computer, print out map directions from MapQuest, or buy DVDs to watch our favorite movies for the 50th time. Thanks to cloud computing, we can access files, real-time driving directions, movies, and much more instantaneously through the internet.

As the largest cloud computing platform in the world, Amazon Web Services, also commonly referred to as AWS Cloud or AWS, has played a vital role in making sure we consume more content via the internet than ever before. Hosting websites and IT infrastructures of countless well-known companies such as Airbnb, Adobe, Disney, Comcast, Capital One, and McDonald's, AWS has been directly impacting our daily lives for years. Being a big player in the IT world as well as our daily lives, AWS and cloud computing are both worth learning about as we get more deeply entrenched in the digital world.

In chapter 2, we begin learning about the different cloud concepts that help differentiate cloud computing from legacy on-premises IT infrastructure (think: physical server rooms and data centers). We discover advantages of cloud computing, types of cloud computing models and deployments, and design principles in cloud computing.

1.3 When should I use or not use cloud computing?

As with any product or service, there are situations where you should or shouldn't utilize cloud computing to solve your IT needs. AWS, as a whole, is considered an *Infrastructure as a Service* (IaaS) platform. We will go more in depth on what IaaS is in later chapters, but in a nutshell, it means that AWS provides all the tools necessary for you to set up and maintain IT infrastructure by helping you customize and build a cloud-based IT infrastructure for a fraction of the cost and time of setting up a physical hardware-based IT infrastructure in your office or data center. As the name suggests, it provides (IT) infrastructure as a service.

1.3.1 When should I use cloud computing?

There are many reasons cloud computing has swept up the technical world like a tornado, influencing everything from government to corporate IT to personal lives. When utilized productively, cloud computing can make IT solutions more affordable, flexible, reliable, and/or efficient than what we used to utilize for our legacy IT infrastructure.

Utilizing cloud computing services can help teams quickly scale their resources, such as compute or database resources, up or down depending on demand. Need more capacity? You can get it almost instantaneously. Need less capacity? Turning it down a notch is almost instantaneous too! And with a pay-for-what-you-use model of billing, you end up paying only for the IT resources you utilized, so you aren't stuck with a huge bill at the end of the month for all the resources you didn't use.

Are you an online shop running a once-a-year mega sale and expecting potential customers rushing to your website to increase by 100-fold? No problem! Your cloud computing platform of choice helps you scale your resources to meet demands instantaneously. This allows your excited customers to flood your online shop without the threat of crashing your website.

Your sale is now over, and the number of customers returns to normal. That'll mean that your increased cloud computing resources are no longer necessary. No problem! You can scale down your resource usage instantaneously so that you don't keep on paying the extra fees associated with the added resources. With physical hardware and infrastructure, it is more difficult to scale your resources up or down, because it would require purchasing expensive equipment that may take a while to arrive and set up. Not to mention, when you no longer need the equipment, you're usually stuck with it.

Another reason cloud computing may be a better choice for your IT infrastructure is the fact that not only can you access a virtually limitless amount of resources almost instantaneously, but you can also rely on its security and reliability. Have you ever lost months' worth of work because of a hard drive failure on your computer or needed an important file for a meeting but misplaced your thumb drive? Perhaps some sensitive documents got lost somewhere on a thumb drive, causing the compliance department to scramble to attempt to retrieve it before a competitor got hold of it. AWS and other cloud computing platforms take the reliability, durability, and security of your IT resources very seriously. As a result, losing or misplacing data becomes a much rarer issue.

Not only can you rely on cloud computing platforms to hold your data securely and confidently, but you can also rely on them to make data access much more convenient in both work life and personal life. If you've ever utilized a service such as Box or Dropbox to store or share files with friends or messaged your colleagues or family on a messaging app such as Facebook Messenger, Google Hangout, or Microsoft Teams, you're utilizing cloud computing to access and share resources and information more efficiently and conveniently than ever before!

Ok, so now we know cloud computing is pretty cool (right?). But why should we be looking into AWS over other large cloud computing platforms such as Microsoft Azure and Google Cloud? Every platform and service provider has different strengths and weaknesses, and AWS is not an exception. And I'm obviously biased, having spent the past few years talking about AWS. However, the most enticing aspect of considering AWS as a cloud IT solution over other cloud computing providers is probably its sheer size, in terms of both market share and breadth of products being offered.

Even if you don't end up utilizing AWS, or you decide to work at a company that uses another cloud computing platform, because of the similarities between AWS services and concepts we discuss in detail throughout this book and their counterparts in other major cloud computing platforms, you will likely have a much easier time getting up to speed with any of them. A virtual server is a virtual server, whether it's called Amazon Elastic Compute Cloud (Amazon EC2) or Azure Virtual Machine.

AWS has steadily held the top market share in the cloud computing platform space since its launch in 2006 and provides services ranging from compute and storage to the Internet of Things, mobile, and even satellites. Thanks partly to its enormous customer base and variety of industries served, AWS is able to provide diverse types of services to fit its clients' needs at very competitive prices. Chances are, your IT and development teams will be able to find a service or a group of services that fulfills their goals by utilizing AWS. If not, at least you can utilize the knowledge you glean from this book to jump-start your cloud computing journey in other platforms.

1.3.2   *When should I not use cloud computing?*

As exciting and innovative as cloud computing can be, it's not always the best solution for your IT problems or needs. Fundamentally, because cloud computing requires you to access IT resources using the internet, if your internet connection goes down, you're in a pickle. If there is a network outage in your area or in the area hosting the data center, there's a problem. In a related vein, if the platform itself goes down, whether due to network issues, massive hardware failures, or worse, the company going out of business, you are in a *massive* pickle.

Another issue that can potentially be a deal breaker for people who need extremely quick access to their IT resources may be the *latency*. Latency in IT is the time it takes for data to get from one place to another. Just as with shipping packages, the farther data has to travel, the longer it takes to arrive. Working on files on your workstation (laptop or desktop computer) has the lowest latency, because you are accessing the files directly on your local hard drive. Working off a *local server* (a server that is housed in your office's server room) may cause a slight delay, but that delay would be much shorter than accessing the same files using the internet (and rarely perceptible for us mere mortals).

In the case of cloud computing, because the data is being accessed using the internet, the speed at which the data can be uploaded or downloaded is heavily reliant on the speed of the internet between you and the data center hosting your resources. For most of us, these differences are almost imperceptible and do not cause workflow issues, but for those who rely on instantaneous updates or resource access because of the nature of their work, these slight delays may be a deal breaker. Having latency over a certain limit may be detrimental for people such as stock brokers who need almost no latency in receiving information and executing stock transactions. These are issues you encounter because you are relying on a company to host your resources in a remote location, which requires a secure and fast internet connection to access.

Another reason you or your company may decide to not utilize cloud computing is the fact that, depending on your location, it may not be available at all or its offerings may be limited. For example, as of the writing of this book in 2022, there is only one AWS Region in the whole continent of Africa (Cape Town) and one in South America (São Paulo). There are none in Russia or North Korea and just one in the huge country of Canada (the second one is coming to Alberta in 2023–2024).

Not only are there certain countries and regions in the world where cloud computing access may not be available, but there are also discrepancies in the types of resources and services offered by location. For example, it is a widely accepted fact that with AWS Cloud, the East Coast and West Coast of the United States are regions that have more variety of services and tend to receive newer services first. Other regions such as Singapore, Sydney, Tokyo, and Frankfurt are also known to have access to a more diverse selection of services.

Some industries and situations may not be as conducive to using cloud computing over legacy on-premises IT infrastructure. An example could be a situation we reviewed earlier, where the users are doing types of work that require virtually zero latency. Another barrier could be compliance issues and security concerns. While AWS has been strengthening its government-servicing branch, hosting government resources will obviously have many different security-related issues and concerns than most non-governmental entities. If all the regulations are not addressed, government agencies are unable to utilize the AWS Cloud. Another industry that has a lot of compliance-related restrictions is the medical industry. Because much of the data stored by medical industries such as hospitals is extremely sensitive in nature, there are many regulations surrounding how and where data can be stored, both in the hospital's own compliance rules as well as at the government level. While rapid progress is being made to onboard the healthcare industry onto the cloud, depending on how the rules are written, many in the medical industry are still unable to store their data in the cloud.

There are many reasons why cloud computing may be a fit for your unique situations and needs, and there may be equally as many reasons why it may not be a fit. It's important to make sure that you are choosing a solution that meets your specific requirements in all different aspects, ranging from financial and regulatory to efficiency and ease of use.

As a side note, when you are on a hunt to solve an IT issue, you may be looking for a *solution* instead of a *platform*. For example, say you are an IT manager looking for an affordable and efficient way of managing your company's emails and file sharing for employees. You *could* cobble together a solution using different services AWS offers. Alternatively, you could sign up for a subscription with Google Workspace (formerly G Suite), and almost instantaneously have access to user management, email, file storage and sharing, instant messaging system, calendar system, and much more.

As we mentioned earlier, AWS Cloud as a whole is an IaaS platform. AWS has many great features and services, but sometimes you're looking for a quick solution to a specific problem you're having and not an entire platform. In those cases, you may opt to purchase a ready-made service offered by another company instead of piecing together a custom solution using different AWS services. While this is definitely not a strike against utilizing cloud computing in general over legacy infrastructure (rather, a potential strike against utilizing a whole platform as opposed to a ready-made solution), it may be food for thought when comparing different cloud computing platforms (IaaS) versus Software as a Service products such as Facebook and Gmail. We discover the different types of cloud computing models in chapter 2.

1.4 Conceptualizing cloud computing and AWS

If what we've been talking about in this chapter seems rather confusing and nebulous, you aren't alone. Creating a mental model of what all of the concepts and terminologies mean, as well as what fits in where, is difficult when tackling cloud computing, with or without an IT background.

1.4.1 Cloud computing, AWS, and you

The most fundamental mental model we want to establish is the relationship between you, the user, and the IT resources that "live in the cloud." Generally speaking, you would access the IT resources hosted on cloud computing platforms, such as AWS, via the internet on your local machine (usually a computer).

As a scenario, let's imagine that your IT department decided to move the graphic design team's digital assets from a *local server* (a server that exists physically in the office) to a *virtual server* (a server that is hosted by a cloud computing platform) on AWS.

Let's take a look at figure 1.1, which shows your home Wi-Fi network's relationship to AWS. I'm going to be throwing out a few service names that may seem confusing, but don't worry! We go over all of them in detail in the upcoming chapters. But for now, let me quickly describe the services I'll be mentioning:

- *Amazon EC2*—Virtual server/virtual machine (think: computer/server in the cloud)
- *Amazon Virtual Private Cloud (Amazon VPC)*—Virtual network (think: virtual version of your home Wi-Fi network)

If you are accessing data on a virtual machine hosted on AWS, you likely have an Amazon EC2 instance, a virtual server, set up inside an Amazon VPC, a virtual network. Amazon VPC creates a virtual version of an isolated computer network so that your resources running in AWS are separated from everyone else's resources.

Think of it like the cloud computing version of your home Wi-Fi network. Your laptop, printer, cellphone, and tablet all "live" within your home Wi-Fi network. Because the printer and your laptop are connected within your home network, you can print files from your computer through the Wi-Fi network. However, unless your neighbor has cracked your Wi-Fi password, they shouldn't be able to print documents from your printer using their own computers. Figure 1.1 helps us visualize the relationship between your home or office Wi-Fi network and AWS, connected via the internet. Your home Wi-Fi network is your own isolated network where you can share data with the devices connected to it as well as access the World Wide Web through the internet. Amazon VPC allows you to create your very own isolated virtual network so that your (virtual) neighbors don't get into your business and see how many cat photos you have saved on your (virtual) server (no judgment).

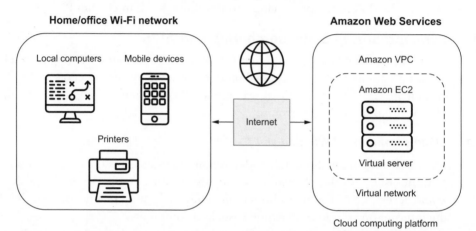

Figure 1.1   Accessing resources on Amazon Web Services via the internet from your own local computer

Cloud computing platforms such as AWS have extremely large *data centers* (buildings filled with a huge number of powerful servers and other IT equipment) all around the world to serve their clients' IT needs via the internet. You, as a user, access files, servers, and countless other IT resources with an internet connection from your computer.

In chapter 3, we introduce AWS's global infrastructure and how it's similar to or different from legacy IT infrastructure. You'll also learn about deploying and operating in AWS by using different deployment methods, such as Infrastructure as Code and AWS Command Line Interface. You'll learn about how the AWS global infrastructure is set up, including concepts such as Availability Zones, Regions, and architecting for high availability.

1.4.2   *Breaking down AWS*

Now that we've established how to access IT resources housed in cloud computing platforms, let's figure out what the relationship is between IT infrastructure, cloud computing, and AWS and its various tools and services:

- *Cloud computing* is a type of IT infrastructure that is accessed by users through the internet.
- *AWS* is a type of cloud computing platform (offered by Amazon) and currently holds the largest market share in the cloud computing world.

AWS offers many services and solutions for your IT needs. These cloud services are broken down into service categories, sometimes referred to as *service groups*. As of the summer of 2022, there are a little over two dozen service groups offering services ranging from compute and storage to robotics and satellites. Let's try to visualize the relationships between these components.

Let's take a look at compute services and drill down in figure 1.2. Compute services provide computing resources through the internet. These could be through virtual machines such as EC2 or serverless services such as AWS Lambda. (We learn about these services in detail in chapter 4.)

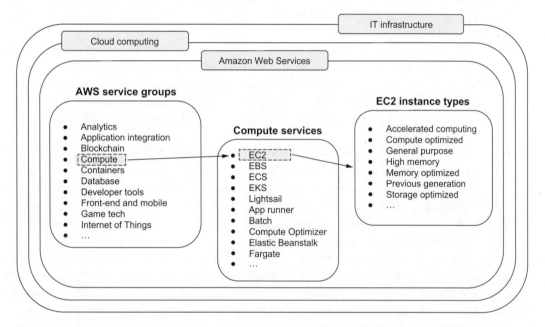

Figure 1.2   Amazon Web Services is a cloud computing platform that has service groups and services.

We want virtual servers! So we select Amazon EC2 as our service of choice. Here, just as with your personal computers, you have options depending on the intended use. Video editors and software developers would choose different types of computers, as would video game streamers versus students who mainly utilize their computers for social media and writing papers. Similarly, you have options for your virtual server that cater to your needs. Do you need to perform heavy computational tasks? You can choose Compute Optimized Instances. Do you need a large amount of space for huge files? You can select Storage Optimized Instances. Do you just need an all-purpose,

Swiss army knife type of virtual server? General Purpose Instances will probably serve you well. While the types of instances being offered change depending on new technological developments on AWS's side, you'll likely find a type of virtual server to fit your specific needs.

When we take an initial look at AWS, the number of services and solutions it offers can take our breath away (over 200 as of mid-2022!). Some of the most popular service groups are computing, storage, networking, database, and developer tools (all coming up in chapter 4). They even have satellites as a service for you to borrow AWS's satellites to do whatever you do with satellites. Some of the most popular services are Amazon EC2, which is a compute service, and Amazon Simple Storage Service (Amazon S3), which is a storage service.

In truth, the number of services AWS provides seems to increase by the day, and even the most vigilant AWS connoisseur likely does not know the most up-to-date numbers and features. And that's OK! Even though AWS has a huge number of offerings, it's quite alright to start out with a few that are personally useful to you and slowly expand your repertoire.

In this section, we learned a bit about Amazon EC2. It's a virtual server solution and one of the most widely utilized services in all of AWS. Throughout this book, and especially in chapter 4, we learn about many more core AWS services one by one. By the end, you'll come out with a fairly good overview of many of the core features and functions of some of the most popular services the platform has to offer you.

1.5 *AWS Certified Cloud Practitioner exam (CLF-C01)*

The *AWS Certified Cloud Practitioner exam* (CLF-C01) is currently the only foundational-level certification exam offered by AWS. This exam is designed to help validate cloud fluency and foundational AWS knowledge of the exam-taker. As the description suggests, it's the perfect certification exam to prove your understanding of the core concepts and services AWS offers its customers.

It's available to be taken online and in testing centers and is offered in 10 different languages. Whether you picked up this book to help you prepare for the AWS Certified Cloud Practitioner exam or not, becoming familiar with the contents outlined in the exam is a great first step in pursuing a future with cloud computing using AWS or another cloud computing platform.

AWS recommends that an ideal candidate come in with at least 6 months of active engagement with the AWS Cloud environment that provides them with exposure to AWS design, implementation, and/or operations. However, I personally have not found this to be necessary in terms of studying for and passing the certification exam. For reference, I spent a few months studying the content, playing around with the AWS console and a few core services following tutorials, and took the exam, with about 3 years of IT experience. However, any actual hands-on learning and tinkering experience accelerates learning and helps you become more comfortable and familiar with the platform, so I highly recommend it!

As a candidate for sitting on this foundational exam, you are not expected to know how to code, design, troubleshoot, implement, or migrate cloud architecture. You are also not expected to execute performance testing or to comprehend business applications for different cloud solutions and services. This means that if you have a good grasp of the content being covered, you can have a crack at the exam.

This exam is a 65-question multiple-choice/multiple-response exam and does not require you to perform any operations in the AWS Cloud environment. It is pass/fail (you either pass or fail). The score scale is 100 to 1000, with a minimum passing score of 700.

You can download the exam guide, try out some practice exam questions, and go over the scope of the exam on AWS's official website (http://mng.bz/BZxw).

1.5.1 The four domains

There are four domains, or content areas, to this exam, all dominating different percentages of the exam. They are as follows:

- Cloud Concepts (26%)
- Security and Compliance (25%)
- Technology (33%)
- Billing and Pricing (16%)

Together, these four domains help AWS validate that you have foundational knowledge about key tools, technologies, and concepts that help you begin your AWS Cloud adventures. Refer to table 1.1 to see the types of content each domain expects you to demonstrate:

- Do you understand the value proposition of having your IT resources in the cloud instead of housing them in on-premises servers?
- What is the Shared Responsibility Model, and how does it divide responsibilities for security of your cloud computing resources?
- Can you identify the core AWS services and what they do?
- How is paying the bill for AWS different from how we generally pay IT bills?

These are some of the questions we will tackle in this book as we go through the four domain areas featured in this certification exam.

Table 1.1 AWS Certified Cloud Practitioner exam

Domain 1: Cloud Concepts (26%)	Domain 2: Security and Compliance (25%)
<ul><li>Define the AWS Cloud and its value proposition.</li><li>Identify aspects of the AWS Cloud economics.</li><li>Explain the different cloud architecture design principles.</li></ul>	<ul><li>Define the AWS Shared Responsibility Model.</li><li>Define AWS Cloud security and compliance concepts.</li><li>Identify AWS access management capabilities.</li><li>Identify resources for security support.</li></ul>

Table 1.1   AWS Certified Cloud Practitioner exam *(continued)*

Domain 3: Technology (33%)	Domain 4: Billing and Pricing (16%)
<ul><li>Define methods of deploying and operating in the AWS Cloud.</li><li>Define the AWS global infrastructure.</li><li>Identify the core AWS services.</li><li>Identify resources for technology support.</li></ul>	<ul><li>Compare and contrast the various pricing models for AWS.</li><li>Recognize the various account structures in relation to AWS billing and pricing.</li><li>Identify resources available for billing support.</li></ul>

1.5.2   *Studying for the AWS Certified Cloud Practitioner exam*

This book is designed to be an introduction to cloud computing and AWS, as well as to provide study materials for the AWS Certified Cloud Practitioner exam. As such, we devote a large section of the book to information and concepts required to pass the certification exam.

Figure 1.3 illustrates where in this book each component of the certification exam is taught:

- In chapter 2, we learn about the first domain, Cloud Concepts.
- In chapter 3, we are introduced to AWS global infrastructure, and in chapter 4, we learn about the core AWS services. Together, chapters 3 and 4 make up the third domain, the Technology domain.
- We learn about security and compliance concepts and services in chapter 5, which makes up the second domain, Security and Compliance.
- To wrap up the four domains, we evaluate Billing and Pricing aspects in chapter 6.
- In chapter 7, we reintroduce the AWS Certified Cloud Practitioner exam and the four domains in more detail, as well as provide study aids and tips for the exam.

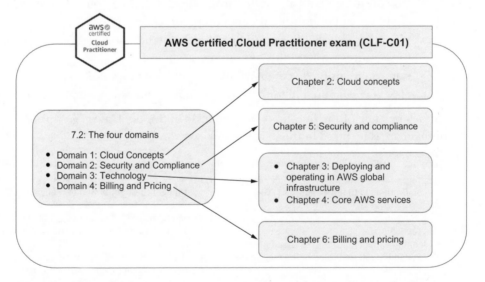

Figure 1.3   Where in the book each component of the AWS Certified Cloud Practitioner exam is explained in detail

Now that we've discussed what cloud computing is, how AWS fits into it, and the AWS Certified Cloud Practitioner exam, let's get right into learning about important cloud concepts that help distinguish cloud computing from legacy IT infrastructure systems in the next chapter.

Summary

- Cloud computing is, according to AWS, the "on-demand delivery of IT resources over the internet with pay-as-you-go pricing."
- AWS (also known as AWS Cloud) is a cloud computing platform offered by the tech giant Amazon.
- Cloud computing alleviates many of the technical, financial, and administrative constraints that come with setting up and running legacy IT infrastructures.
- There are situations where an IT operation benefits greatly from shifting to cloud computing, but there are also many situations where IT operations are better off staying on-premises (on-site).
- Cloud computing is a type of IT infrastructure that is accessed using the internet, and AWS is a type of cloud computing platform.
- AWS is broken down into service groups, which are types of services categorized based on their characteristics.
- Each service group has services, which are the specific products AWS offers its customers.
- The AWS Certified Cloud Practitioner exam is a foundational-level exam offered by AWS and helps to validate overall knowledge of the AWS Cloud.
- The AWS Certified Cloud Practitioner exam has four domains: Cloud Concepts (26%), Security and Compliance (25%), Technology (33%), and Billing and Pricing (16%).
- This book is written for those who are interested in taking the AWS Certified Cloud Practitioner exam and those who are not.

Introduction to cloud concepts

This chapter covers

- Introducing cloud concepts
- Identifying advantages of cloud computing
- Defining types of cloud computing models
- Discussing the types of cloud computing deployments
- Examining the pillars of the Well-Architected Framework

In the previous chapter, we were introduced to cloud computing and Amazon Web Services (AWS), as well as the AWS Certified Cloud Practitioner exam. In this chapter, we dive right into learning about cloud concepts, which help us define the value proposition of cloud computing over legacy information technology (IT) infrastructure—or what we consider traditional IT infrastructure. You can think of legacy or traditional IT infrastructure as a room filled with a lot of servers, monitors, and networking cables. It's what movies and TV shows generally portray as the "IT room."

In this chapter, we learn about the six advantages of cloud computing, three types of cloud computing models, three types of cloud computing deployments, and design principles in cloud computing. By the end of this chapter, we'll know why cloud computing has swept the IT world by storm over the last decade and how it's different from the legacy IT systems that we used in previous decades.

2.1 Cloud concepts introduced

There are some defining characteristics of cloud computing that differentiate it from what we consider legacy IT infrastructure. What does legacy IT infrastructure look like? Imagine server rooms in offices filled with servers and network cables or off-site data centers in their own secluded, secured buildings that hackers in popular TV crime shows target to steal top-secret corporate information or bring down access to important IT resources to cripple the company (I'm channeling USA Network's *Mr. Robot* scenes here).

Legacy IT infrastructure costs a lot of money to set up and maintain, and it is not very flexible to changing requirements. Just setting up a server room or off-site data center requires a considerable amount of time, labor, and, again, money.

Cloud computing revolutionized what it means to run IT infrastructure. To help us better understand the value propositions of cloud computing, AWS has summarized some key benefits, design principles, and economics of cloud computing in what it calls *cloud concepts*.

Cloud Concepts is also the second largest domain in the AWS Certified Cloud Practitioner exam and helps to convey the value propositions of cloud computing over legacy IT infrastructure.

The cloud concepts we discuss are as follows:

- Six Advantages of Cloud Computing
- Three Types of Cloud Computing Models
- Three Types of Cloud Computing Deployments
- Six Pillars of the Well-Architected Framework

2.2 Advantages of cloud computing

For any new technology, the advantages of using it over other similar products must be made extremely apparent before widespread adoption. We tend to be reluctant to change our ways, and it's difficult to get people to change their minds on processes when "it's always been done this way." If you've ever encountered a management team that seems very set on keeping very inefficient workflows because it's "just how we do things here," you're probably familiar with the frustration this mentality can sometimes cause.

Why should we shift from using the tried-and-true Microsoft Word to Google Docs when Microsoft Word has been working just fine for years? Do I really want to learn how to use a different operating system from scratch when I've been using a Mac with no problems for a decade, and I know all the shortcuts to make my workflows efficient? Figure 2.1 shows one such example over the past few decades: why make the switch to a complicated smartphone when a landline phone worked perfectly well to make calls?

To help convey the value proposition of cloud computing, AWS has come up with the "Six Advantages of Cloud Computing." They are as follows:

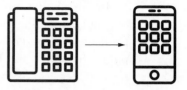

Figure 2.1   Why make the switch from traditional landline phones to smartphones when the call function works perfectly well on traditional phones?

- Trade capital expense for variable expense.
- Benefit from massive economies of scale.
- Stop guessing capacity.
- Increase speed and agility.
- Stop spending money running and maintaining data centers.
- Go global in minutes.

Let's go over them one by one to see what these catchy phrases mean.

2.2.1   *Trade capital expenses for variable expenses*

Paying for IT resources works differently with cloud computing than for many more traditional IT purchases. With cloud computing, companies are charged for their IT resources more like an electricity or utility bill rather than as an upfront purchase order. For a finance department unfamiliar with the way cloud computing resources are billed, there may be a lot of confusion in the beginning.

CONSIDER THIS . . .

John works in the finance department of a manufacturing company, and the IT manager requests budget approval of a new IT purchase. As usual, John asks the IT manager the specifics about what is being purchased and how much it costs.

"Well," the manager says, "part of it's servers, but it's actually more like a whole entire IT infrastructure. And I can give you an estimate on how much it'll cost, but not the actual dollar value, because it's charged more like a monthly utility bill, rather than having a purchase price. So we don't know the exact dollar amount until the month is over, because we won't know how many resources we used until then."

John isn't sure how to proceed. He's used to monthly bills for electricity and office rent, but a fluctuating monthly bill for servers? That's a new one.

OUR SOLUTION

The IT manager argues that the company will save money because instead of incurring a huge capital expense up front for IT hardware that may or may not fit its needs in the long run, the expenses will be smaller and vary month to month based on the resources used to exactly fit the company's needs. "Think of it similarly to our office's operational expenses month to month," says the IT manager.

Capital expense (CapEx), or *capital expenditure*, is a financial concept that refers to money that is required to acquire, improve, or maintain physical assets. When you need to replace all of your corporate laptops because your company keeps a 3-year life cycle for computers (all computers get replaced every 3 years), that's a capital expense.

Generally, to acquire, improve, or maintain infrastructure or assets, you need a lot of money at once and pay for it in advance, and once the products are in your possession or construction has begun, the infrastructure is not very flexible to changing demands. In our server room example, purchasing IT equipment is a capital expense because the company pays a lot of money, likely up front, to acquire the assets necessary to build it.

Another feature of running a successful organization is managing *operational expenses* (OpEx). Operational expenses are expenses that a company incurs while conducting normal business operations. These costs include, for example, rent, office supplies, maintenance fees, insurance, and utilities. In IT, these expenses may also include software licensing fees, leasing printers from a vendor (and paying for their maintenance contracts), internet subscriptions, and utility fees associated with keeping the IT infrastructure running (and cooled).

> ### Curious about estimating your IT architecture's costs on AWS?
> You can use the AWS Pricing Calculator to create a cost estimate that fits your business needs utilizing AWS products and services! The AWS Pricing Calculator is available at https://calculator.aws/.
>
> Chapter 6 is filled with different AWS cost calculators and tools to help you budget your AWS resource usage bills.

Now, let's consider *variable expenses*, which refer to expenses that change based on the activities performed or received. Some examples of variable expenses are shipping costs by volume or distance and the monthly electric or water bill. With the variable expense method of payment, you pay for what you use, when you use it.

Going back to the server room example, with cloud computing, instead of creating and maintaining a physical server room in your office, you can create *virtual servers*—servers that are created virtually using a cloud computing platform—on AWS using services such as Amazon Elastic Compute Cloud (EC2; we discuss the Amazon EC2 in detail in chapter 4).

You can almost instantaneously have virtual servers custom-configured for your specific needs with very low upfront costs. As you can see in figure 2.2, with variable expenses, instead of paying for the outright purchase of physical servers, you are paying for how much computational resources you consumed on the cloud computing platform month to month while using these virtual servers.

By utilizing cloud computing instead of an old-school IT setup, you can trade a good chunk of your capital expenses for variable expenses, as if you are paying your

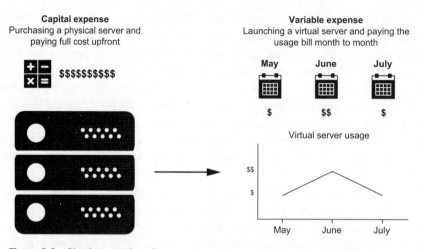

Figure 2.2 Cloud computing allows you to replace capital expenses (a large amount of money up front) with variable expenses (pay-as-you-go), so you pay only for what you used as a monthly bill.

monthly water bill based on your water usage. Gone are the days when you had to make big-money decisions before you knew exactly how many resources you needed. Now, you can pay for resources you consume only when you consume them.

2.2.2 *Benefit from massive economies of scale*

When we begin evaluating whether or not to purchase something, one of the biggest factors in our decision-making is the cost. For corporate purchases, these financial decisions are magnified a hundredfold, as the volume of purchases is so much larger. Just as office managers save money on office supplies such as toilet paper, coffee, and paper towels by buying them in bulk from wholesalers, IT managers can save money on IT resources by taking advantage of cloud computing platforms that act like wholesale stores.

CONSIDER THIS . . .

You are a freelance video editor and have been creating numerous promotional videos for an important product launch. You need to make sure everything is saved, including different versions of the same video, but you're quickly running out of space on your computer and your external hard drives (you also need to be constantly backing up your data to avoid catastrophic data loss).

Each external hard drive costs several hundred dollars, and it's getting rather unwieldy to have so many external hard drives cluttering your office. Not to mention, it's a pain to find that one specific video you're looking for in a pinch. You wonder if there isn't a more cost-effective and convenient way to store data so you can focus on creating amazing promos instead of how much storage space is left on your devices.

OUR SOLUTION

Cloud storage services such as Dropbox, Box, and Google Drive have done wonders for our data storage needs in the past decade. They allow us to store large amounts of data on the cloud and access them from anywhere that has an internet connection. This means that you, as the video editor, can quickly send the link to your most recent draft to your customer for approval instead of spending time figuring out the best way to send large files.

AWS and other large cloud computing platforms have massive data centers filled with an extremely large number of powerful servers. Given that these enormous companies with very generous budgets can buy powerful resources in bulk, they benefit from massive economies of scale, because in many instances, they pay less per unit by purchasing in larger quantities.

By using cloud computing platforms, you can rent virtual resources for less than if you attempted to purchase the physical hardware yourself. As figure 2.3 illustrates, AWS and other cloud computing platforms purchase their computing resources in huge quantities, allowing them to provide these resources for lower fees. Thanks to their massive economies of scale, AWS and other cloud computing platforms can offer lower pay-as-you-go prices, thus passing on the savings to their customers, which means we also pay less for what we use.

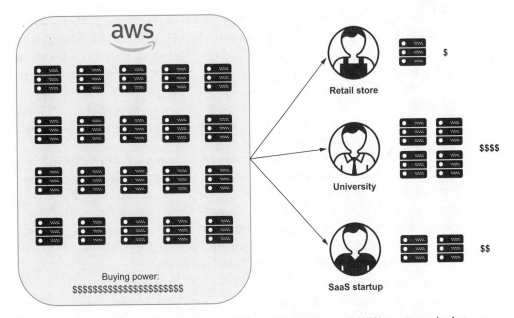

Figure 2.3 We benefit from the massive economies of scale because of AWS's enormous buying power that can purchase huge amounts of IT resources for cheaper per-unit costs.

As a video editor, instead of having to spend hundreds of dollars buying new external hard drives every time you run out of space, you can pay a few dollars extra on your monthly storage subscription to have access to gigabytes of additional storage.

2.2.3   *Stop guessing capacity*

Whether it's grandma's secret recipe or corporate IT resources, accurately assessing how much of what you need to get the job done is an ongoing issue. Making a mistake with a recipe means it won't come out as delicious as you'd hoped, and not being able to accurately predict your business resource needs in IT means you may run out of space on your server or, alternatively, have too much. It's also difficult to adjust once you've committed to a plan of action. For a recipe, you can run to your closest grocery store for last-minute chocolate chips, but with expensive IT equipment such as servers, you could be looking at a hefty price tag to fix your incorrect assumptions.

Guessing capacity for IT resources is a source of headaches for companies and finance departments around the world. I can't look at an office building and make a rational guess about how much the monthly electricity bill would be. Guessing capacity for IT resources is similar. Thankfully, cloud computing platforms make guessing capacity a thing of the past, allowing us to more quickly adjust when we realize that we need more or less than anticipated.

CONSIDER THIS . . .

The accounting department needs a new server for the company's new payroll system. Because the company is rapidly expanding after a big round of funding, management isn't sure how many people they will end up hiring. The company will end up eventually paying all of its new employees using the new system. It's important to make sure the new server will not run out of storage space because the company has hired new people, which will require using more data. At the same time, the company doesn't want to overcompensate by buying an extremely expensive server with a huge amount of storage, risking wasting money and resources.

Even though the company isn't quite sure how much data storage will be required to run the payroll system, the accounting department needs something working immediately. The system needs to be up and running to process payroll for current employees while ensuring that when needs change, accounting can almost immediately adjust its resources. Purchasing physical servers when you aren't quite sure how much storage you need can be problematic, as having too little or too much capacity can mean a lot of wasted time, money, and resources.

OUR SOLUTION

With cloud computing, the amount of resources such as storage and memory that you require for your servers is flexible and less expensive than purchasing a physical server. Need more memory because you're running a heavy program? No problem! We'll add some with a few clicks. Need more storage space because you're running out? No problem! We'll add some in just a few minutes. Without having to make a guess about how many resources you may need for a specific project, you can utilize virtual servers that can flexibly adjust to fit your needs when your requirements change.

Estimating your IT infrastructure's capacity needs is difficult. Even if you estimated your resource needs correctly and purchased the optimal resources, situations can change at a drop of a hat. You may have too much capacity because you bought servers that are too high-spec, or you may not have enough capacity because you quickly outgrew the available resources. In both cases, you may end up spending more time, money, and resources to rectify the issue than previously anticipated.

Figure 2.4 shows a decision tree for the purchase of a new computer when utilizing the traditional procurement process. You have many things to consider, such as the amount of storage, memory, and processing power you may want in your computer, as well as practical things like how large you want the computer to be and how much you can afford. With all these options in mind, you make a choice and purchase a computer.

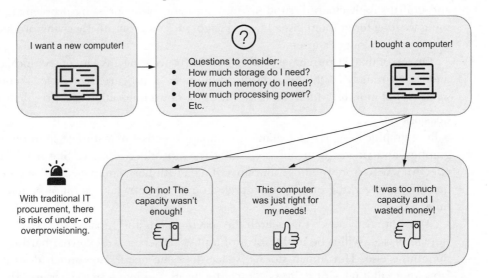

Figure 2.4   Traditional IT procurement runs the risk of under- or overprovisioning your IT resources, which can be costly to remedy.

When you make the purchase, we can consider three possible outcomes:

- The capacity of the computer you purchased wasn't enough for the job you had in mind.
- The capacity of the computer you purchased was just perfect for the job you had in mind.
- The capacity of the computer you purchased was overkill, and you wasted money.

With traditional IT procurement, you run the risk of under- or overprovisioning your resources, which can lead to wasted money, time, and/or labor.

With cloud computing, you can stop guessing capacity and access as much or as little resource capacity as you need. When you need extra resources, you can get them within minutes. When you no longer need those extra resources, you can shut them down. Instead of spending a lot of money up front to buy a server with capacity that may or may not meet your needs, you have access to as much as you need, only when you need it. And, of course, you only pay for the resources you used, when you used them.

2.2.4   *Increase speed and agility*

The standard corporate procurement process generally takes a considerable amount of time and human labor to make the purchase. In the last few years, the global pandemic has made this process even slower as impacts range far and wide. It has led to large-scale chip shortages (important for any computers, smartphones, tablets, etc.) and global supply chain disruptions (among many other pressing problems). Something we took for granted just a few years ago, such as promptly receiving orders from overseas, is no longer a given.

On top of that, IT purchases tend to have hefty price tags, as a lot of technical equipment is extremely costly. As a result, traditional IT procurement cycles could take weeks, if not months, which can drastically slow down innovation and productivity.

CONSIDER THIS . . .

Sally, a graphic designer at a vitamins company, needs a new storage solution for the graphics and videos her team is creating for a product rebrand. She needs a cost-effective way to store the huge amounts of data with her teammates, and she needs it quickly. However, the procurement cycle at her company takes a bit of patience and time.

To begin, Sally needs to research the specifications and capacity she requires for a storage device. Will it be in the form of a physical server, an external hard drive, or something else? How much storage space does she need? How much does it cost? How long will it take for delivery? Once she decides which device she wants, she must submit the procurement request to her manager for approval.

There may be a lengthy approval process because of the high cost of the new equipment, which may go up and down her department's chain of command as well as the finance department. There may also be contracts and service agreements that need to be negotiated with vendors. Finally, after months, she receives the delivery of the storage device, and while she's setting it up, she might realize that in the past few months requirements changed, and this storage device is no longer optimal for her team's needs. Now what? She must go through the entire procurement process all over again!

OUR SOLUTION

If Sally had taken advantage of an available cloud computing storage solution, the whole process might have only taken her an afternoon, from research, to request for approval, to the budget approval. Because many cloud computing storage solutions allow you to pay for only what you use, when you use those resources, the fees are much lower than purchasing a physical device outright. As the amount of storage she uses goes up or down, Sally can quickly adjust her storage plan. As a result, the service provider will automatically adjust her bill, so she does not have to worry about running out of storage and having to go through another procurement process to purchase a larger storage device.

As illustrated in figure 2.5, cloud computing helps to increase the speed and agility of IT operations because new or additional resources are generally only a few clicks away. Accessing IT resources from cloud computing service providers is much cheaper and faster than procuring a physical server or other costly IT equipment.

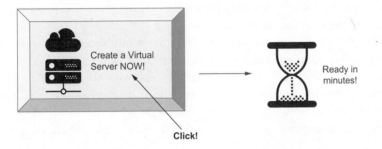

Figure 2.5   Cloud computing allows us to increase speed and agility, spinning up IT resources almost instantaneously instead of waiting for weeks or even months to receive and set up physical equipment.

Making additional resources available to your developers and employees can go from weeks (or even months) down to just minutes. When more or fewer resources are necessary, adjustments are also speedy. The agility of an organization is dramatically increased in the process, because the cost, labor, and time it takes to experiment and develop new features are significantly reduced.

2.2.5 *Stop spending money running and maintaining data centers*

A *server room* is a room full of servers (yes, really). The room itself is usually colder than other rooms in the office to keep large numbers of servers and other IT equipment from overheating (electronics devices create heat!). There are other IT resources in the room that help to run a robust and healthy IT environment for the organization, such as data storage devices (think: very large external hard drives) and uninterruptible power supplies (they provide emergency power when electricity gets cut off, commonly referred to as UPSs). When an entire building is devoted to housing and maintaining servers and other IT resources, it is called a *data center*.

As you may expect, creating, running, and maintaining server rooms and data centers is very expensive. There's rent for the extra office space or an entire building, as well as the necessary renovations to make the space appropriate for a large amount of heat-producing equipment. There are human capital costs of hiring and training staff to set up and maintain the equipment, as well as pure operational costs, such as electricity usage and replacing broken parts or equipment. Perhaps most important, there is the cost of the expensive IT resources themselves, such as the servers, UPSs, and data storage devices. In all, having your own data center or server room is very cost- and labor-intensive.

CONSIDER THIS...

You are a CFO of a small yet rapidly growing startup to revolutionize the ride-sharing industry. Until now, the organization was small enough that you made do with Google Workspace, using Google Drive and Gmail to share information with your employees and clients. However, your company will be onboarding engineers to begin product development in earnest, which means that your new engineers will need dedicated servers and other resources to pursue their work.

As the CFO, you want to give them what they need but also be cognizant of the costs associated with setting up IT infrastructure. Since the office you rent right now is small, you may end up moving to a bigger office space as your company grows. At that point, you'll have to budget for a new server room, including renovations, in addition to an office move. Is there a way to give your engineers what they need while cutting the financial and human-labor costs associated with setting up and running a server room?

OUR SOLUTION

Setting up, managing, and staffing server rooms and data centers take a lot of time, money, and labor. By choosing to host your IT resources in a cloud computing plat- form instead of a physical IT infrastructure housed in a server room, you can save a considerable amount of time, labor, and money. You and your engineers no longer need to worry about setting up and maintaining the physical aspects of server rooms or data centers and can instead focus your energy on creating innovative products and solutions for your customers.

If you host your IT infrastructure in the cloud, when your office moves, your IT resources move with you without the need to set up a new server room from scratch. Instead of spending money running and maintaining data centers and server rooms, your company will be paying a monthly bill that charges you only for the IT resources you utilized the previous month.

By allowing AWS or another cloud computing platform to worry about the physical IT infrastructure associated with data centers, you can spend more time and resources wowing your customers with your innovations instead of worrying about the literal and figurative heavy lifting of setting up and managing these IT infrastructures.

2.2.6 *Go global in minutes*

Just a decade or two ago, when the internet was slower, web developers had to get fairly creative to make sure all of their images, videos, and data loaded successfully and efficiently onto their users' browsers. They tried techniques such as slicing images and placing them next to each other to reduce loading time. Waiting for videos to buf- fer before pressing Play so you could watch more than 15 seconds of every clip was the norm. These days, we expect everything to load instantaneously and be available the moment we click a link.

In the past decade, high-speed internet services have allowed us to consume data and information like never before. While it seems to occur seamlessly, people and resources are working behind the scenes to make sure we don't have to wait more than a few seconds to load the next episode of our latest Netflix binge.

CONSIDER THIS . . .

Jack is a project manager at an online teaching platform hosting video content that teaches busy professionals skills they need to upgrade their careers. The learning platform serves students from around the world, and the company needs to make sure that anyone who is accessing its content can download and view its videos with as little time lag as possible.

Shipping physical products takes longer if they must come from halfway across the globe when compared to products shipped from a nearby city. Likewise, *data latency*, or the time it takes for data to load, becomes an issue when the person trying to download Jack's videos is physically located far away from the data center hosting his content.

OUR SOLUTION

With cloud computing, we are able to deploy applications and websites in multiple regions and areas around the world in just a few minutes. If you are based out of London, United Kingdom, but someone who wants to access your content is based in Tokyo, Japan, it can take a bit of time before the customer can load your data if your content needs to be downloaded from a server housed in the UK.

By using cloud computing, these applications and websites are cached in data centers in different parts of the world. *Caching data* means that a copy of the data is saved in different data centers around the world so that your customers can receive their information quicker by downloading the saved data from a data center physically closest to them. Because the data does not have to travel as far, the information loads quicker.

Before the internet, to have a global presence, your company needed to have a physical presence in different continents and countries. Now, as long as your target audience can access the restrictions-free internet, you can communicate with and sell to just about anyone in the world. I can sell my eBook to someone in the United States, Japan, and South Africa all from one website and spend my days talking to people from different parts of the world on social media. Because the data I am sharing with my customers or followers are cached in data centers in various parts of the world, we can communicate with each other and consume data with minimal time lags.

Figure 2.6 shows how cloud computing allows you to benefit from the power of the internet to quickly deploy your applications in multiple regions around the world with just a few clicks. Within minutes, your product is online and globally accessible. Have a product update you want to deploy globally? A few clicks, and it's done! You can provide your customers, wherever they are located, with better and faster experiences at a minimal cost to you.

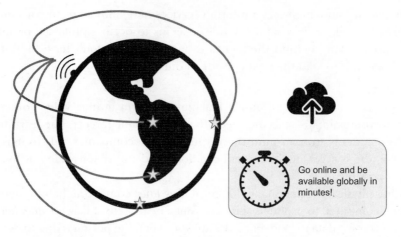

Figure 2.6   Your content can be accessed globally within minutes when utilizing cloud computing.

2.2.7   Section quiz

Company B is a new startup that finally gained enough traction to rent an office space. It wants to spend as little time, money, and human labor as possible setting up and maintaining its IT infrastructure so employees can focus on developing and innovating the company's product—a mobile app that helps students find other students from around the world to virtually study together. Which of the following advantages of cloud computing helps the company to accomplish its goals?

   a   Trade capital expense for variable expense.
   b   Stop spending money running and maintaining data centers.
   c   Increase speed and agility.
   d   Go global in minutes.
   e   All of the above.

(Find the answers to this quiz and subsequent quiz questions at the end of each chapter in "Chapter quiz answers.")

2.3   Types of cloud computing models

Every cloud computing user has different needs and requirements. An engineer might want a way to set up databases very quickly to analyze data sets. A DevOps engineer might need to create an entire IT infrastructure in the cloud for their company and wants to control every aspect of the environment. A writer might want to quickly set up a blog with the least amount of hassle so they can get down to writing without needing to worry about the underlying technical architecture that is running the blog.

Fortunately, there are cloud computing services for practically every technical need and level of expertise, ranging from full-service end-user applications like Twitter to open-ended IT infrastructure such as AWS's Amazon Virtual Private Cloud, a service that creates virtual networks (like your office Wi-Fi network) to house your virtual IT resources (we learn about this and many other essential services in the following chapters).

These different use-case scenarios are broken up into three types of cloud computing models:

- Software as a Service (SaaS)
- Platform as a Service (PaaS)
- Infrastructure as a Service (IaaS)

Figure 2.7 provides a bird's-eye view of what type of need each cloud computing model may serve.

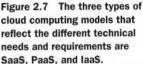

Figure 2.7 The three types of cloud computing models that reflect the different technical needs and requirements are SaaS, PaaS, and IaaS.

Knowing the distinctions between the three models will help you to understand what type of structure and support a cloud computing service provider is offering and which option may work best for your needs, as shown in figure 2.8.

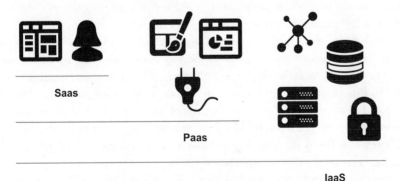

Figure 2.8 The type of cloud computing model you choose to use may depend on how much technical control you want and how much technical expertise you want to outsource to the service provider.

When you want to quickly create and publish a blog website, you may select an SaaS product. When you want to customize your blog's theme (layout), look at analytics, or utilize different plug-ins or widgets, you may use a PaaS service. When you want to control all aspects of your website, including the networking, databases, servers, and security, you may pick an IaaS platform.

2.3.1   *Software as a Service*

Log into Facebook to shoot off some messages to friends. Upload your home renovation progress pictures onto Dropbox to share with your family. List a new piece of hand-made jewelry on Etsy, and log into WordPress.com to publish a blog post talking about it. All of these are examples of the SaaS model of cloud computing.

SaaS provides products managed by the service provider. Utilizing a SaaS product means that you don't have to worry about the underlying IT infrastructure or how to maintain and manage the services. In most cases, they are end-user applications, which means all you have to worry about is how to use, and benefit from, that product or software.

In the case of your web-based email service, such as Gmail, you can send and receive emails without worrying about creating or maintaining the web-based application, how the server is managed, or the uptime of the IT infrastructure housing the whole system. SaaS products are great for services you'd like to use as an *end user* (a person who uses, rather than manages, a product), instead of being concerned about creating and managing the underlying IT infrastructure.

2.3.2   *Platform as a Service*

You've decided to start a blog to talk about your passion: cats. There are so many things to research and write about! You decide to go with WordPress, an SaaS service, so you can focus on the end-user experience of writing and publishing your articles.

A few months later, you realize that your cat blog is getting quite a bit of traction, so you want to invest in a better layout and explore different plug-ins to enhance your blog. You are also interested in the analytics—seeing where your visitors are coming from and which posts are popular. To help monetize the cat blog, you want to sell cat merchandise to your visitors and hope to embed an online shop feature into the blog. When you hire a WordPress developer to help you create a unique layout with custom features, including the ecommerce function, the developers are working with a PaaS.

PaaS provides an environment for engineers to create and deploy applications without being concerned about building or maintaining a complex backend infrastructure. They can focus on building products or functions instead of configuring and managing servers, databases, and data centers.

WordPress can function as an SaaS platform when you create a blog out of the content management system. As a user of the SaaS blogging platform, you can worry about writing and publishing awesome blog posts and very little else. WordPress can also function as a PaaS when developers get involved to build different features and functions into the blog. For example, with your cat blog, you can embed an ecommerce service that already exists (such as utilizing the Shopify plug-in), or an engineer can create a custom-made online shop.

While you or your engineer can customize and add many functionalities that don't exist in the SaaS usage of WordPress, when you utilize it as a PaaS, you still are not involved with the infrastructure side of running the blog, such as setting up and maintaining a physical or virtual server to host your blog.

PaaS is great for engineers and organizations who want a little more control over their environment than what SaaS products provide but don't want to worry about managing a complex IT infrastructure. This allows engineers to build applications more efficiently, because they can spend all their energy on the code and development instead of the underlying IT infrastructure.

2.3.3 Infrastructure as a Service

Your company is ready to have its entire IT infrastructure on the cloud and eliminate its physical server room. While there are many SaaS or PaaS services that provide solutions for different parts of your IT needs as a company, there isn't one that allows you to configure and maintain a virtual version of your server room.

You want the convenience and cost-effectiveness of cloud computing but still want to configure and customize your IT infrastructure to your heart's content. Want to use storage, networking, servers, and compute resources while retaining flexibility and control of setting up and maintaining your own IT infrastructure? What you are looking for isn't a service or a platform but an infrastructure. AWS, Google Cloud, and Microsoft Azure are examples of IaaS models.

IaaS refers to the physical or virtual IT infrastructure that a cloud computing service provider offers, including supplying compute, storage, networking, and other IT resources on an on-demand or pay-as-you-go basis. The customer has a variety of resources to configure and utilize, including network, storage, and server services. IaaS allows customers to build and maintain a cloud-based IT infrastructure for a fraction of the cost and time that would be required to set up physical hardware infrastructures and data centers from scratch.

Configuring and maintaining an IaaS environment requires more engineering expertise than utilizing an SaaS or PaaS cloud computing model. However, when looking for flexibility and customizability without sacrificing cost-effectiveness or convenience, IaaS may be the cloud computing model of choice.

2.3.4 Section quiz

AWS Lambda is an AWS service that helps users run code without needing to manage servers. It allows developers to run code for virtually any kind of application without worrying about the infrastructure management. This resource is an example of which of the following cloud computing models?

  a PaaS
  b IaaS
  c SaaS

2.4   *Types of cloud computing deployments*

Just as you have flexibility with how much control you want over your virtual IT infrastructure by choosing a cloud computing model that works for your expertise and needs, you also can deploy cloud computing infrastructures in different ways to fit your unique needs. In IT, *deploying* refers to the process of setting up computer and network systems so they are ready for use.

With cloud computing, the different types of deployment refer to the different ways you can set up your IT infrastructure so it's ready for use. As with cloud computing models, cloud computing deployments differ in how much control you have over the system. A lot also has to do with where your IT infrastructure will reside. The three types of cloud computing deployments are as follows:

- Cloud/cloud native
- Hybrid
- On-premises

2.4.1   *Cloud/cloud-native deployment*

Cloud deployment, or cloud-native deployment, is what many people imagine when they think about cloud computing. All parts of the application or the infrastructure are deployed, or "live," on the cloud. Users access these resources on the cloud via the internet. These applications can be created in the cloud or be migrated onto the cloud from existing physical infrastructure (for example, moving data from your computer's hard drive to Dropbox).

When we compose our text on WordPress's text editor, edit some photos on Canva, and publish a blog post, the whole process of updating our blog is utilizing cloud deployment. You get the full benefit of cost, labor, and time savings that comes with cloud computing when you use cloud deployment.

2.4.2   *Hybrid deployment*

Although cloud computing comes with many benefits, one downside is that your information travels through the internet. The fact that data travels through the internet is not an issue in most cases, thanks to improvements in data transfer speeds in recent decades. However, when dealing with extremely large amounts of data on the cloud, the lag can become noticeable. Sometimes, a business can rely so much on the data that any lag can be problematic for its day-to-day operations. This is where hybrid deployment may come in.

An example of hybrid deployment in action is setting a folder on your computer to automatically sync to Dropbox so you always have a backup of your files online. Because you have the original copy on your computer, you can edit your videos without experiencing lags, but you can feel safe knowing a copy is stored in the cloud in case something happens to your computer's hard drive. On a corporate scale, companies can have their employees work from local copies (files saved to their hard drives), and their system can be set up to automatically sync to the cloud after 5:00 p.m. so that the whole company has a daily backup in the cloud.

Hybrid deployments are also often used when companies are in the process of moving their data onto the cloud but have not yet completed the process. Hybrid deployment connects cloud-based infrastructure with existing resources that reside on physical computers and servers on-site.

2.4.3 On-premises deployment

Sometimes referred to as *private cloud*, on-premises deployment is the deployment of resources on-premises, or on-site, which utilizes virtualization and resource management tools offered by cloud computing. *Virtualization* is the act of creating a virtual version of something. In the case of cloud computing, servers and computers are often created as virtual machines. This means that you can use these computers and servers as though you are using a physical computer or server, but they exist as software instead of hardware.

Since everything is local, or on-site, and not uploaded to the cloud, it's a little harder to see the benefits of cloud computing when you use on-premises deployment. From the outside, everything might look very similar to a legacy, or traditional, IT infrastructure that we are familiar with from the precloud era. Companies utilizing on-premises deployment may still have their physical server rooms and data centers.

You can conceptualize on-premises deployment as utilizing the technologies of cloud computing (such as virtualization and resource management) in a physical IT infrastructure. As you might expect, you don't receive the full benefits of cloud computing technologies with a private cloud.

But enough benefits exist that it is one of the three core cloud computing deployment types available. One such benefit could be that the risk of security compromises may be reduced because on-premises deployment allows organizations to fully control and maintain their own networks for the infrastructure, as no part of the infrastructure "hits" the public internet.

Companies may prefer to keep their data on-premises for security reasons but still want to use the virtualization and application management resources cloud computing offers to increase resource utilization in their IT infrastructure. In places where going fully or even partially on the cloud is not possible because of various restrictions, on-premises deployment may be a way to gain some benefits of cloud computing but keep the legacy IT infrastructure intact.

2.4.4 Section quiz

A company is in the process of moving data from its physical servers onto the cloud. While it is doing the heavy lifting of transferring gigabytes of data into AWS, it is utilizing a mixed cloud computing deployment approach where part of the data is on the cloud, and the rest remains on the company's physical servers. This is an example of _____ deployment.

a   on-premises

b   hybrid

c   cloud/cloud-native

2.5   *Pillars of the Well-Architected Framework*

The Well-Architected Framework is considered the best-practices framework for building the most secure, fault-resilient, efficient, and high-performing cloud IT infrastructure. In basic terms, it's the best way to create your IT infrastructure in the AWS Cloud to make sure it's safe, reliable, and cost-effective. Following these recommendations for best practices will help your organization create a more stable and cost-efficient IT environment so you can focus on developing your services and products. AWS defines the framework with six best-practices pillars.

As illustrated in figure 2.9, these pillars of the Well-Architected Framework are as follows:

- *Operational excellence*—Daily system operations, monitoring, and improvements
- *Security*—Protecting information and systems
- *Reliability*—The ability to prevent and quickly recover from operational failures
- *Performance efficiency*—Using computing resources efficiently
- *Cost optimization*—Avoiding unnecessary costs
- *Sustainability*—Minimizing environmental impacts of cloud workloads

Six pillars of AWS's Well-Architected Framework

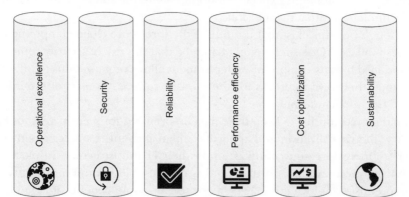

Figure 2.9   The six pillars that make up AWS's Well-Architected Framework are operational excellence, security, reliability, performance efficiency, cost optimization, and sustainability.

As we go over the key elements and questions to consider, keep in mind that most of these scenarios and actions are probably not something you will encounter in your day-to-day operations if you are not the systems administrator or a high-level stakeholder in the IT department of your organization. However, it is good to reflect on these questions as you consider how operational excellence, security, reliability, performance efficiency, cost optimization, and sustainability for your organization's cloud IT infrastructure will help run the business more efficiently and smoothly.

2.5.1   Operational excellence

The best kind of workdays in IT are days filled with calm and predictable procedures rather than chaos and unexpected events (queue emergency alert emails and panicked scrambling to figure out what's wrong). Preventing incidents from happening, writing good documentation, and, when inevitable incidents do occur, learning from mistakes and improving documentation are some ways IT departments can strive to improve their day-to-day operations.

As shown in figure 2.10, the operational excellence pillar helps organizations create and maintain reliable IT infrastructure by recommending that the way IT is run

- supports business objectives;
- creates effective day-to-day operations;
- gains insights into daily operations via monitoring;
- updates documentation when changes are necessary;
- investigates events and improves procedures.

Achieving operational excellence is *iterative* (continuous improvement), which means that efforts to improve your IT infrastructure's operations never end.

Operational excellence pillar

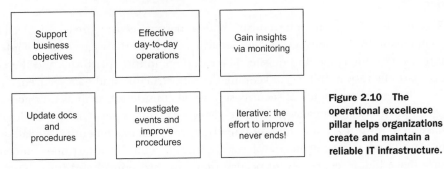

| Support business objectives | Effective day-to-day operations | Gain insights via monitoring |

| Update docs and procedures | Investigate events and improve procedures | Iterative: the effort to improve never ends! |

Figure 2.10   The operational excellence pillar helps organizations create and maintain a reliable IT infrastructure.

The key elements of the operational excellence pillar are as follows:

- Change automation
- Event responses
- Defining standards for managing daily operations

The operational excellence pillar of the Well-Architected Framework focuses on how to best support business objectives and priorities, run day-to-day operations effectively, gain insights via monitoring, and continue to improve processes and procedures. Operational excellence is never-ending and iterative. You can't just "set it up perfectly" and call it a day. The operation must be monitored and improved continuously to make sure it's running smoothly and efficiently.

An organization is set up for success by having well-defined and shared goals, with every branch in the organization understanding its part in achieving the desired business outcomes. Every operational failure or event needs to be investigated and thought of as an opportunity for improvement. As lessons are learned and applied, the organization becomes more and more effective at supporting its business objectives.

QUESTIONS TO CONSIDER

- Have you set up monitoring services on your IT resources so if some important server or network goes down, you're immediately notified?
- Are day-to-day operations documented and constantly updated as you improve your processes?
- Do you make frequent, small, and reversible changes to your resources instead of large changes that are difficult to reverse if something goes wrong?
- When an unexpected event occurs, does the team come together to do a *postmortem* (examination of what went wrong) and then update procedures and documentation to reflect any learnings so it doesn't happen again?
- Do you anticipate failure and perform *premortem* (opposite of postmortem) exercises so that potential points of failure can be identified and dealt with before actual failures occur?

2.5.2 *Security*

Recently, it seems as though we hear about a massive security breach of a well-known company or entity almost every day. Security is an important part of an IT infrastructure both on the cloud and on-site. The cloud computing platforms and the customers share the responsibilities of keeping the infrastructure and data secured.

Different components of security should be considered, such as user access management (don't share passwords; force password changes periodically; don't give permission to resources a user does not need), resource management (keep data secured in transit and at rest; protect all layers of infrastructure, not just one), and making sure that when a security event occurs, there are procedures and traceability put in place to figure out what went wrong and prevent it from happening again. We just introduced a lot of new security considerations, so let's go over what some of these concepts mean.

As shown in figure 2.11, the security pillar of the Well-Architected Framework recommends that you

- Utilize strong identity controls.
- Automate security event responses.
- Protect all layers of your IT infrastructure (not just one or two).
- Encrypt and protect data (at rest and in transit).
- Be mindful of the principle of least privilege.

As we saw in the operational excellence pillar, the effort to improve security is an iterative one—it never ends!

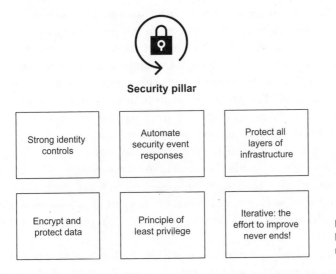

Figure 2.11 The security pillar helps organizations create and maintain secure IT infrastructure.

The key elements of the security pillar are as follows:

- Security of data
- Identity management and controls
- Protecting systems
- Detect security events

Understanding the key principles for the security pillar of the Well-Architected Framework helps to create an IT infrastructure that is more resilient to security events such as leaked data or hacking. Security of IT resources is an extremely important concept that requires constant attention and review.

Like operational excellence, security in the cloud is an ongoing and iterative process. When incidents occur, they are opportunities to enhance the IT environment's security. Striving to have strong identity controls, automating security event responses, protecting all layers of the infrastructure, and managing data with encryption are some core security principles that should be implemented in all IT environments.

Identity controls refer to user and entity access management. It controls who logs in where, what they have access to, and what they are able to do. Users should not be sharing log-in credentials, passwords should be changed periodically, and when someone no longer needs access to certain resources, the access should be cut off immediately.

These considerations tie in directly to an important security concept called the *principle of least privilege*. In the most fundamental sense, the principle of least privilege dictates that you should only provide access to resources and information as needed. For example, everyone in the company shouldn't have access to payroll or other human resources information. Likewise, the whole IT department probably does not need to be able to log into the backup server when an engineer is present who is responsible for maintaining daily backups of corporate servers. Information and resources should be made available only for legitimate reasons, and when the person or entity no longer requires access, the permissions should be immediately changed to reflect that.

When a security event, such as a data breach or compromised credentials, occurs, having automated security event responses helps your organization tackle the issues quickly and efficiently. Instead of relying on humans to notice and respond to security events, having automated responses allows your tracking and monitoring systems to kick in and patch or fix certain issues as soon as the system notices them.

An example of an automated security event response may be a monitoring software realizing that you have a "public bucket" in Amazon Simple Storage Service (Amazon S3) and automatically changing the permissions to make the bucket private. Amazon S3 is a cloud storage solution, which can be thought of as a sophisticated version of storage services like Dropbox or Box. You can store files in S3 buckets (folders) and access them for different needs.

Like a file you store in Dropbox, you can make the folders and files public or private. In most instances, resources stored in corporate Amazon S3 buckets should not be public, as they often contain sensitive information. As such, the IT administrator can set up an automated security event response using certain AWS security and monitoring services to alert them when a public bucket is detected within the corporate AWS infrastructure. The automation will then switch the bucket setting to private. In the meantime, having received the monitoring alert, the IT administrator can go find the engineer who made the bucket public and confirm that it was intentional.

The automation allows the IT administrator to move immediately to confirm the incident rather than scrambling to make the bucket private. If the bucket was made public intentionally for a legitimate reason, the IT administrator can change the setting back to public. If not, something that could have caused catastrophic damage to the company was avoided, thanks to the automated security event response!

In a similar vein, enabling *traceability* to monitor alerts and logs that tell you who did what and when is important, as knowing where the breach happened and why will help administrators make sure that similar future breaches do not occur. While it's important to prevent security events from occurring, when they inevitably happen, having alerting systems set up to swiftly notify administrators and, if automated, automatically make changes can prevent these events from remaining unnoticed for longer than necessary.

Figure 2.12 demonstrates how you should secure all layers of your infrastructure, which will make it much harder for hackers to get to your information. You can visualize this by imagining how much safer your emails are from prying eyes if you have multiple layers of protection, such as password protecting your home Wi-Fi network and your computer as well as your email account, rather than just password protecting your email account.

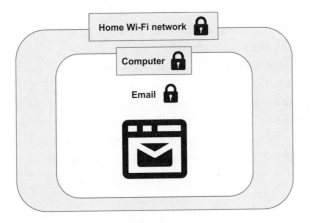

Figure 2.12   You can more fully secure your emails by having multiple layers of protection.

Another important concept in the security pillar is that you must protect all layers of your cloud infrastructure, not just one layer of it. If you have your Wi-Fi network secured with a password, your computer secured with a different password, and your email secured with yet another, it is much more difficult for hackers to gain access to your emails than if only one of your layers was secured. Likewise, there are multiple layers to IT infrastructure, and every layer must be secured and protected to make it harder for one password or one access point to allow a hacker to gain access to the resources you're trying to protect.

We can't complete our thoughts about security and IT infrastructure without talking about the resources and data we are protecting. Your data should be protected at rest (while it's housed somewhere, such as on your hard drive or cloud storage) and in transit (while it's moving from one location to another, such as via email or file transfer). Encryption should be used wherever possible, and storage solutions should be configured with care to make sure an event such as the Amazon S3 bucket situation doesn't accidentally happen. You may need to remind your coworkers to be mindful of where they save or send sensitive corporate information or files.

Keeping IT infrastructure, resources, and data safe is everyone's responsibility and is not just the concern of the cloud computing platforms or the IT department. Employee awareness is crucial to sustaining a healthy security pillar. In chapter 5, we discuss more security-related concepts in detail, including the shared responsibility model and the principle of least privilege.

- Does every person have unique log-in credentials into the system? No one is sharing accounts or passwords?
- If a user no longer needs access, is their access to resources cut off immediately?
- Are routine password changes mandatory to eliminate long-term static passwords?
- Are you practicing the principle of least privilege (give permissions only when necessary)?
- Is traceability enabled by setting up monitoring alerts and logs so you know who made what changes from where and when?
- Are you securing all layers of infrastructure, not just one layer?
- Is data protected in transit and at rest?
- Are security best practices automated using software, and are people kept away from data so the risk of mishandling data due to human error is reduced?
- Are you prepared for security events with policies and processes so when a failure occurs, there's a speedy and effective investigation and recovery?

2.5.3 *Reliability*

If you want to hire a professional to solve an important issue for you, you will likely hire someone you consider reliable. When these reliable professionals run into new issues, they use their experiences and problem-solving skills to attempt to help you. Reliable people can be trusted to get work done consistently, and it's the same with reliable IT resources and infrastructure.

Figure 2.13 shows the different ways your IT resources can become more reliable, according to the reliability pillar of the Well-Architected Framework. Your IT infrastructure can become more reliable by

- setting up automatic recoveries upon failures;
- utilizing distributed system design;
- using updated recovery procedures;
- requiring consistency in performance;
- architecting for resiliency.

Echoing many other pillars, the effort to create a reliable IT infrastructure is iterative and is never over.

Key elements of the reliability pillar are as follows:

- Distributed system design
- Recovery planning
- Handling changes

Without the reliability pillar of the Well-Architected Framework, you cannot trust your resources to carry their weight in responsibilities. If you can't trust your server to be up at all times, you can't create services for your customers who rely on that server to be functioning. While it's impossible to expect 100% uptime for IT resources, there

Reliability pillar

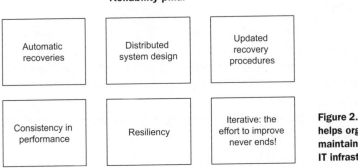

Automatic recoveries	Distributed system design	Updated recovery procedures
Consistency in performance	Resiliency	Iterative: the effort to improve never ends!

Figure 2.13   The reliability pillar helps organizations create and maintain reliable and consistent IT infrastructure.

are ways to mitigate potential issues and failures by setting up automatic recoveries, maintaining updated recovery procedures, and reducing the impact of a single failure on the infrastructure as a whole.

Your organization can strive to reduce the impact of a single point of failure, such as a disconnected server, on the infrastructure as a whole by utilizing a distributed system design. The IT infrastructure would be set up so that there are multiple small resources serving a purpose rather than one large resource hosting everything. If one small resource fails in a distributed system, it will not become a single point of failure for the whole infrastructure because the other small resources will provide resiliency.

One of the most important factors for reliability in the cloud is resiliency. *Resiliency* refers to the resource's ability to recover from disruptions, as well as its ability to mitigate disruptions. Resiliency in a system also allows it to easily adjust and acquire computing resources to meet fluctuations in resource demands. An online shop may have a surge in customers accessing its website for its annual sale. A resilient system would automatically realize there is an increase in demand and make sure to acquire more server space and memory to withstand the influx of customers visiting the website. Without this resiliency, the website may go down soon after the start of the sale from an overload of requests and enthusiasm.

QUESTIONS TO CONSIDER

- Is your organization's IT able to perform its intended functions efficiently and consistently?
- Are you able to test and operate the workload throughout its entire life cycle (from beginning to end)?
- If a failure occurs, are your resources set up to automatically recover to a working state?

- Are you testing recovery procedures so that when something does occur, you're well prepared to tackle the issue?
- Are you utilizing distributed system design so one server's failure doesn't bring down the system as a whole?

2.5.4 *Performance efficiency*

Both in our personal lives and in the business world, efficiency in getting tasks completed is key. Enhancing performance efficiency usually means you are using the right tools for the job, evaluating which methods work best for your specific situations, and adjusting methodologies when needs change so that you are consistently utilizing the optimal resources.

As shown in figure 2.14, to achieve performance efficiency, the Well-Architected Framework recommends that you

- Select appropriate tools for the jobs.
- Monitor the performance of your architecture.
- Use serverless architecture where possible.
- Utilize team members efficiently.
- Focus on agility.
- Make changes as requirements evolve.

Performance efficiency pillar

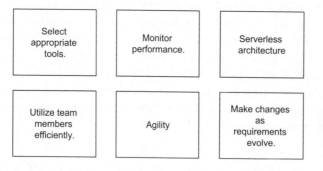

Figure 2.14 **The performance efficiency pillar helps organizations to create and maintain efficient and high-functioning IT infrastructure.**

The key elements of the performance efficiency pillar are as follows:

- Select the right resource types and sizes to meet your requirements.
- Monitor performance.
- Make changes to maintain efficiency as the requirements evolve.

The performance efficiency pillar of the Well-Architected Framework focuses on increasing the agility and performance of your team and resources. *Agility* in IT refers to how efficiently an organization and its IT infrastructure can respond to external pressures to change when needs arise. An efficient IT system can meet changes in demands and utilize cloud computing resources efficiently to meet goals and requirements. Staying current with the constant updates to the AWS Cloud allows your organization to take advantage of different ways to maintain a high-performance IT infrastructure.

While the efficiency of cloud computing resources' performance relies on how the infrastructure is designed, the human resources side of performance efficiency also warrants attention. If knowing the complex ins and outs of a specific technology is not a priority for your team, you may consider outsourcing those configurations to a vendor so that your engineers can focus on your products and services, which will help to improve the efficiency of your team.

Another way your business can outsource expertise and focus on what really matters for your organization's products is by utilizing *serverless architectures*. Serverless architectures allow organizations to remove the operational burdens of managing physical IT infrastructure, which may save your company money, labor, and resources.

While we learn more about the concept of serverless architecture in a little more detail in chapter 4, in a nutshell, it consists of services or resources that allow you to run your code or workloads without the need to set up or maintain your own servers. AWS has a set of services that allow you to use serverless computing, including AWS Lambda, Amazon S3, Amazon DynamoDB, and Amazon Aurora Serverless.

NOTE If you are interested in learning a bit more about serverless services at AWS, you can check out this link: https://aws.amazon.com/serverless/.

If you use a serverless architecture with AWS, your applications still run on servers, as if you are operating your own servers, but the server management is taken care of by AWS. Even if you are utilizing Amazon EC2, you are still going to be spinning up a virtual server that you are responsible for patching and managing. With serverless architecture, you don't have to worry about that.

Utilizing serverless resources means that your team does not have to worry about provisioning, scaling, or maintaining servers to run applications, databases, or storage systems. Instead, you can focus on developing and innovating your products, making the development process more efficient.

QUESTIONS TO CONSIDER

- Do you use serverless architectures to remove the operational burdens of managing physical IT infrastructure?
- Do you use virtual resources to test and experiment with different technologies to find the most efficient and effective configurations before committing?

- Do you delegate the complicated technical operations to your cloud computing service providers so that your engineering team can focus on development of your products and services instead of learning and managing complex and specialized technologies?
- Are your resources deployed in multiple regions around the world to provide lower latency for your customers?

2.5.5   *Cost optimization*

The health of a business is often directly tied to the financial health of the business. To keep a business running smoothly financially, the money coming in and the money going out have to be constantly monitored and evaluated. To minimize expenses without compromising business needs, companies must spend time figuring out how to best meet their requirements without overspending or sacrificing quality.

As figure 2.15 shows, the recommendations for achieving cost optimization for a well-architected IT infrastructure are fairly similar to having good personal finance habits. The cost optimization pillar of the Well-Architected Framework recommends that you

- Analyze spending over time.
- Avoid unnecessary costs.
- Attribute expenditures to owners (who is utilizing which resources).
- Scale to meet needs without overspending.
- Don't overcompensate when choosing resources (don't overprovision or overpurchase services that are not necessary because of the fear of underprovisioning).

Echoing many of the other pillars, the process of cost optimization for your IT infrastructure is iterative and never-ending.

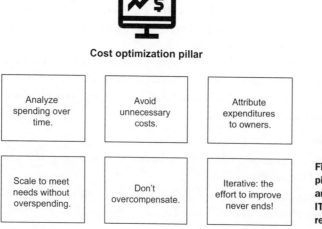

Cost optimization pillar

Analyze spending over time.	Avoid unnecessary costs.	Attribute expenditures to owners.
Scale to meet needs without overspending.	Don't overcompensate.	Iterative: the effort to improve never ends!

Figure 2.15   The cost optimization pillar helps organizations create and maintain a cost-effective IT infrastructure that meets requirements without overspending.

The key elements of the cost optimization pillar are as follows:

- Understand and control where and how money is spent.
- Select the most appropriate resources for the requirements.
- Analyze spending over time.
- Scale resources to meet needs without overspending.

The core concept for the cost optimization pillar of the Well-Architected Framework is to avoid unnecessary costs and pick the most appropriate resources for business requirements and needs. Traditional IT infrastructure with physical devices and resources required predicting future requirements, which made it more difficult to accurately purchase resources that met demands both in the present and in the future.

The nature of cloud computing helps to alleviate some of the pain points associated with selecting the most appropriate resources for current needs, as well as scaling resources up or down in the future as requirements change. By being cognizant of the cost optimization pillar, your organization can maximize its return on investment.

As with many of the other pillars in the Well-Architected Framework, cost optimization requires continuous refinements and improvements to make sure your company is avoiding unnecessary costs while still meeting business requirements and goals.

Analyzing spending over time and *attributing expenditure* (linking resource spending) to its *owners* (people who are using the resources) are some ways you can monitor spending and invite your team to be more responsible for optimizing resource use to help reduce costs for the company. One way your team can help to reduce unnecessary costs is to shut down or stop unutilized resources so that your company is only paying for resources that are necessary at the moment.

Cost optimization takes planning, and in a pinch, many companies tend to overcompensate by buying more resources than they actually need. This can lead to overprovisioned and underoptimized resources, which can mean money being wasted on unused cloud resources. Spending some time and effort up front to create a cost-optimization strategy helps organizations take advantage of all the financial benefits of utilizing cloud computing.

QUESTIONS TO CONSIDER

- Do you shut down or stop unused resources so that you are only paying for computing resources you need and consume?
- Are you taking advantage of the benefits of cloud computing that allow you to remove the operational costs of setting up and managing data centers and server rooms?
- Are you analyzing cloud computing spending over time to evaluate different ways to optimize costs?
- Are you attributing expenditures to owners to help them be responsible for optimizing their resource usage costs?
- Do you invest time and resources to implement effective cloud financial management so your organization has the necessary knowledge to be cost-efficient?

2.5.6   *Sustainability*

Evaluating the ecological global impact of our actions, monitoring climate change, and looking for ways to build and innovate with sustainability in mind are some concepts we, as modern humans, have been grappling with for decades as global warming and environmental destruction are leading our one planet into potentially irreparable demise. The sustainability pillar of the Well-Architected Framework is a new pillar that was just announced at AWS re:Invent 2021. According to the United Nations World Commission on Environment and Development, *sustainable development* is defined as "development that meets the needs of the present without compromising the ability of future generations to meet their own needs." According to AWS, cloud computing providers have lower carbon footprints and are more energy efficient than typical on-premises environments because they invest in efficient power technology, operate energy-efficient resources (such as servers), and achieve high server *utilization rates* (utilizing as many resources as they have available).

> **NOTE** Interested in learning more about sustainability from the United Nations? Check out the following link: http://mng.bz/deog.

As figure 2.16 shows, the recommendations for optimizing for sustainability are to

- Utilize the shared responsibility model for sustainability.
- Understand the impact of your IT actions on the environment.
- Maximize utilization to minimize resource usage and reduce downstream impacts.
- Apply best practices to help reduce environmental impact.
- Quantify impacts throughout the entire workload life cycle.

As with many of the other pillars, optimizing for sustainability is a continuous effort, focused on energy reduction and efficiency.

Sustainability pillar

Shared responsibility model for sustainability	Understand impacts of services used.	Maximize resource utilization.
Apply best practices to reduce impact.	Quantify impacts through entire workload lifecycle.	Continuous effort for optimization

Figure 2.16   The sustainability pillar helps organizations create and maintain a more environmentally friendly technical ecosystem by focusing on energy reduction and efficiency.

The key elements of the sustainability pillar are as follows:

- Focus on energy reduction and efficiency across all components of a workload.
- Achieve maximum benefit from provisioned resources to minimize the required total resources.
- Cloud architects should understand the environmental impacts of services used to quantify their impacts throughout the entire workload life cycle.
- Each workload deployed by the customer generates a fraction of the total AWS emissions.
- Responsibility for the environmental sustainability of cloud resources is shared between AWS and the customer.

The core focus of the sustainability pillar is to minimize the environmental impacts of running cloud workloads. We must recognize that whatever resources we spin up or consume on the cloud computing platforms consume real-life resources, including electricity and water at data centers, and contribute to producing waste, including deprecating equipment such as servers.

The shared responsibility model for sustainability states that the responsibility of striving for environmental sustainability for cloud infrastructures is shared between the customer and AWS. AWS explains the two responsibilities:

- AWS is responsible for the sustainability *of* the cloud.
- The customer is responsible for the sustainability *in* the cloud.

Some of AWS's responsibilities, such as being responsible for the sustainability of the cloud, may be optimizing the global infrastructure such as data centers, electricity supplies, and building materials, as well as resources used within data centers such as servers, water, waste management, and cooling systems. Some examples of responsibilities that the customer has are data design and usage, software application design, platform deployments and scaling, data storage, and code efficiency.

Some organizations can go a step further and strive for sustainability *through* the cloud. Sustainability *through* the cloud refers to organizations' attempts to utilize AWS technology to solve a broader sustainability challenge, such as reducing carbon emissions or waste, lowering energy consumption, or recycling water. By utilizing data from AWS services designed to help your sustainability efforts, you can detect abnormal behavior, conduct preventive maintenance, and reduce the risk of environmental incidents.

AWS also shares some design principles for sustainability in the cloud, which should be applied to cloud workloads to maximize sustainability and minimize the environmental impact of your cloud IT infrastructure. These are as follows:

- Understand your cloud workload's current and future impact and evaluate ways to improve productivity and reduce impact over time.
- Establish sustainability goals for each cloud workload to help you support the wider sustainability goals of your business.

- Maximize utilization by using right-size workloads, which will help you ensure high utilization and maximum energy efficiency of the underlying hardware by design.
- Anticipate and adopt newer and more efficient hardware and software resources by supporting your partners' and suppliers' attempts at improvements that will help to reduce the impact of your cloud workloads.
- Utilize managed services, which share services and resources across a large number of customers, to reduce the amount of infrastructure needed to support cloud workloads.
- Reduce the amount of energy and resources required to run your cloud workloads, such as eliminating the need for customers to upgrade devices to use your services, which will help to reduce your downstream environmental impacts.

As with many of the other pillars, the process of achieving optimized sustainability for your IT resources requires continuous improvements. Your goals for improvements may be to eliminate low utilization of resources or idle/unused resources or to maximize the value from consumed resources. The process of optimizing may take many iterations, but the ultimate goal is to utilize all of the resources you provision and to complete the same cloud workload with the minimum resources possible to reduce the environmental impact of your cloud IT resources.

QUESTIONS TO CONSIDER

- Are you selecting efficient programming languages and adopting modern algorithms in your development to reduce environmental impacts?
- Do you use efficient data storage techniques and deploy to the most appropriately sized and efficient compute infrastructure?
- Do you minimize usage for high-powered end-user hardware?
- Are you applying best-design practices to reduce environmental impacts?

2.5.7   *Section quiz*

Which of the following is *not* a pillar in the Well-Architected Framework?

  a Security pillar
  b Operational excellence pillar
  c Distributed systems pillar
  d Efficiency pillar

Summary

- Cloud concepts are a collection of fundamental concepts that helps you begin to understand how cloud computing works and how it may be different from legacy, or traditional, IT infrastructure.

- Cloud Concepts is one of the four domains featured in the AWS Certified Cloud Practitioner exam.
- The six advantages of cloud computing are as follows: trade capital expense for variable expense, benefit from massive economies of scale, stop guessing capacity, increase speed and agility, stop spending money running and maintaining data centers, and go global in minutes.
- The three types of cloud computing models are SaaS, PaaS, and IaaS.
- The three types of cloud computing deployments are cloud/cloud native, hybrid, and on-premises.
- The six pillars of the Well-Architected Framework are operational excellence, security, reliability, performance efficiency, cost optimization, and sustainability.

Chapter quiz answers

- 2.2.7: e. All of the above.
  - *Answer*—Company B will benefit from all of the advantages of cloud computing by spending as little time, money, and labor as possible to set up and maintain its IT infrastructure. The six advantages of cloud computing will help it focus on developing and innovating its products quickly and affordably rather than setting up and utilizing legacy IT infrastructure.
- 2.3.4: a. PaaS
  - *Answer*—AWS Lambda is an example of PaaS, where developers and engineers can create and deploy applications without having to worry about building or maintaining complex IT infrastructure.
- 2.4.4: b. Hybrid
  - *Answer*—Hybrid deployment connects cloud-based infrastructure with existing resources that reside on physical computers and servers on site, allowing companies to retain some of their data on site but still take advantage of the benefits of cloud computing.
- 2.5.7: c. Distributed systems pillar
  - *Answer*—The six pillars of the Well-Architected Framework are operational excellence, security, reliability, performance efficiency, cost optimization, and sustainability. Distributed system design is the concept of mitigating infrastructure failure by avoiding the creation of a single point of failure.

Deploying and operating in AWS global infrastructure

This chapter covers

- Hosting information technology infrastructure on AWS
- Defining methods of deploying and operating in AWS
- Introducing the AWS global infrastructure

In chapter 2, we were introduced to *cloud concepts*, which are foundational concepts about the value proposition of cloud computing over legacy IT infrastructure, and how cloud computing works. In this chapter, we learn about hosting an IT infrastructure on AWS, and the different ways you can deploy and operate your IT infrastructure in AWS.

3.1 Hosting IT infrastructure on AWS

The decision to host your company's IT infrastructure on the cloud rather than on-premises in your own server room or data center requires that you learn a new set of concepts and vocabularies to have a successful migration. In this chapter, we discuss AWS in particular, although with a few tweaks in the jargon, you can map similar concepts to other cloud computing platforms such as Google Cloud Platform and Microsoft Azure.

The two large infrastructure concepts we learn about in this chapter that pertain to hosting your IT infrastructure in AWS are as follows:

- Deploying and operating in AWS
- AWS global infrastructure

Understanding how to deploy and operate in AWS and becoming familiar with the AWS global infrastructure are both vital components of the Technology domain of the AWS Certified Cloud Practitioner exam.

3.2   Deploying and operating in AWS

Deploying in IT refers to how we bring the IT resources and infrastructure into action. In the case of cloud computing, it often refers to the IT infrastructure being built up in the cloud computing platform and then being put into action. *Operating* in IT refers to the actions and activities associated with operating the deployed resources on a day-to-day basis. Once resources are *deployed*, they are then *operated* until they are shut down.

We learn about the many ways AWS offers its customers to deploy and operate IT resources in the AWS Cloud platform. In essence, we examine how you can communicate with the AWS Cloud and how you can utilize the AWS Cloud.

3.2.1   Interacting with the AWS Cloud

AWS offers a few different ways for you to interact with the AWS Cloud, ranging from *programmatic access* via running commands in AWS software development kits (SDKs) to utilizing *graphical user interfaces* (GUIs) such as AWS Management Console. (I know, I know, all these new terms! Stick with me for a bit!)

Programmatic access allows you to invoke, or cause, actions through a third-party tool or program. When you share an article you just read on Twitter via the Share This button, you're utilizing programmatic access to post to your Twitter feed. Some ways that AWS offers programmatic access to its resources are through the AWS Command Line Interface (CLI) and AWS SDKs.

Graphical access allows you to take actions on objects displayed on a GUI. AWS offers the AWS Management Console for graphical access to AWS. This type of access is probably the most familiar to us, as we interact with GUIs on a daily basis when we are utilizing most software and websites. Open Facebook to check out some posts and leave some comments. You're utilizing graphical access!

While on the surface we may be communicating with AWS in different ways (for example, clicking around in the AWS Management Console versus using the command line to execute commands), at the core of every interaction with AWS is the Application Programming Interface (API). *APIs* are sets of defined rules that dictate how computers or applications communicate with each other. While there is a lot to learn about APIs and how *API calls* and *API responses* are made, we discuss the basics so that you can conceptualize how they work on a very high level.

Figure 3.1 diagrams how an API call works at a sky-high level. A client application (that's probably your web server) makes an API call, requesting certain information. In this case, you are creating a web application that publishes a Twitter user's 50 most recent tweets to your website. Your API call is like a phone call you make to the Twitter server, asking for the information. Then, the receiving server (that's the Twitter server) sends back an API response with the requested information (the 50 most recent tweets by a certain Twitter user). The data is transferred via the API back to the requesting client application (your web application). Your web application now has the information it wanted, and the transfer of data via API is complete. With these new concepts under our belt, let's get started with the different ways you can communicate with the AWS Cloud.

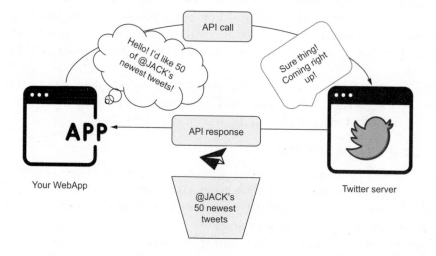

Figure 3.1   Your web application sends an API call requesting certain information, and the Twitter server sends an API response back with the requested information on a very high level.

> **NOTE**   Want to learn more about how APIs work? AWS has a beginner's guide just for you! Check out "What is an API?" here: https://aws.amazon.com/what-is/api/.

AWS MANAGEMENT CONSOLE

You can think of graphical interfaces as anything you utilize on a daily basis on your technology devices, ranging from your phone's AndroidOS to your MacBook's MacOS. If you are able to click or drag objects displayed on a screen, you're likely using a GUI. A GUI presents different ways actions can be performed on objects by the user.

AWS offers the AWS Management Console as its graphical interface. Figure 3.2 is a screenshot of the AWS Management Console with the Services tab in full view, showing you a list of different types of services AWS offers. (Keep in mind that as the technology sector evolves extremely rapidly, this screenshot from Spring 2022 will likely be outdated fairly quickly, but it gives you a visual of what the GUI of an AWS Management Console looks like.)

The AWS Management Console is the website portal that you sign into when you go to aws.amazon.com. You are able to navigate the platform, provision IT resources, and control many aspects of your AWS Cloud infrastructure through the AWS Management Console without touching a single line of code.

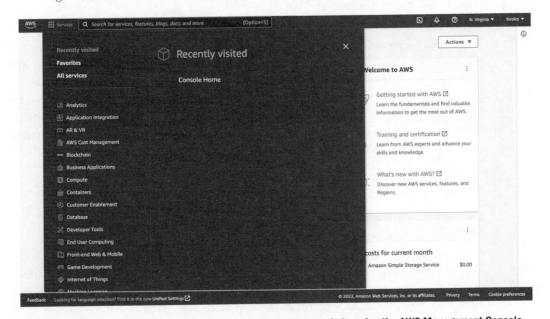

Figure 3.2   You can interact with AWS without typing out commands by using the AWS Management Console, which is a GUI.

When you are first starting with AWS, you will likely begin by getting comfortable with the AWS Management Console. If you have a moment now, I highly recommend that you create an AWS account and begin poking through the Management Console.

> **NOTE**   Looking to learn more about what the AWS Management Console can do? You can check out the documentation for different features of the console at https://aws.amazon.com/console/.

AWS COMMAND LINE INTERFACE

The AWS CLI is a single tool that you can download and configure to control many AWS services from the command line. You communicate with AWS through the AWS CLI by running commands that utilize the API. Once you have created a specific script to do a certain task (such as renaming all files in a directory), you can automate these tasks by running the same script instead of writing out the command each time you want the task completed.

CLIs exist on your computer as well. In Windows, it's called a command prompt, and on a Mac, it's called Terminal. These are user interface applications that are navigated via typing commands instead of using a mouse like the GUIs. Like the Terminal app or Windows Command Prompt on your computer, you can use the AWS CLI to navigate the AWS Cloud with just a keyboard.

> **NOTE** You can download and read the documentation for utilizing the AWS CLI by going to https://aws.amazon.com/cli/.

AWS SOFTWARE DEVELOPMENT KITS

AWS SDKs help developers get the data they are looking for more efficiently by providing coding language-specific APIs for AWS services. As of 2022, the languages AWS supports with AWS SDKs are JavaScript, Python, PHP, .NET, Ruby, Java, Go, Node.js, and C++. As with the AWS CLI, information is requested and received from AWS using APIs. By utilizing the ready-made APIs for various coding languages with AWS SDKs, developers can use the libraries of API calls instead of having to code them from scratch, saving them time and resources.

> **NOTE** You can find out more about AWS SDKs by accessing https://aws.amazon .com/tools/ and finding the SDKs section.

AWS INFRASTRUCTURE AS CODE

Infrastructure as Code (IaC) is the concept that you can deploy and manage IT infrastructure through code, as if you are creating applications as a software developer. These IT infrastructure resources can be networks, virtual machines, load balancers, or anything that helps to maintain a functional IT infrastructure. Using code to manage infrastructure allows organizations to make easily reproducible configurations that drive consistency in environments.

Imagine your favorite pot roast recipe you inherited from your grandmother. Many tries and hours probably went into developing the recipe over generations, but because the best iteration was written down, you don't have to continue trying to replicate it using your instincts. You can follow the directions outlined in the recipe, and you get the exact taste you love that your grandmother grew up with.

IaC allows you to create IT infrastructure like your favorite recipe. Because you are not leaving settings and configurations up to human whims, once you have a setup you like, you can continue to make replicas of that setup over and over by running the same code. The key to consistency in IT architecture is to avoid manual configurations. AWS IaC allows you to enforce consistency across the whole IT infrastructure by leaving the provisioning and deployment to code rather than to manual flicks of the switch.

For AWS, the built-in service that allows you to utilize IaC for your cloud infrastructure is called *AWS CloudFormation*. You can use AWS CloudFormation to create a template that describes the resources you want to create in your AWS infrastructure, and AWS CloudFormation makes it a reality! We discuss AWS CloudFormation in more detail in the next chapter, where we learn about core AWS services.

3.2.2 Deploying in the AWS Cloud

We learned about the methods of utilizing the AWS Cloud in section 2.4. You may recall that there are three types of cloud computing deployments:

- Cloud/cloud native
- Hybrid
- On-premises

Let's quickly review the three types of cloud computing deployment.

Cloud deployment, or cloud-native deployment, is what most people imagine when they think about cloud computing. The entire IT infrastructure lives on the servers of the chosen cloud computing platform, and you access these resources using the internet.

Hybrid deployment is often used when a company is in the process of moving its data fully onto the cloud to make cloud deployment a reality but has not yet completed the process. It is also often utilized when a company sets up automatic backups from its servers or employee computers on a predetermined, consistent schedule to have up-to-date copies of important data in the cloud. It connects cloud-based infrastructure with existing on-premises IT resources, allowing a company to utilize both cloud computing–powered and on-site physical IT resources together.

On-premises deployment is sometimes referred to as a *private cloud*. It is hard to grasp the value of utilizing on-premises deployment when we are talking about cloud computing. It seems counterintuitive to use cloud computing when all IT resources are housed in physical data centers and server rooms on-site. However, cloud computing platforms can still offer benefits such as virtualization to companies that use an on-premise IT infrastructure.

3.2.3 Connectivity options in the AWS Cloud

While we learned about different ways you can *communicate* with the AWS Cloud in section 3.2.1, there are also a few different ways you can *connect* to the AWS Cloud. Connectivity options are ways you can establish network connections to create the highways of data transfers back and forth between your local device and the AWS Cloud. Some of the options that are especially relevant when considering sitting for the AWS Certified Cloud Practitioner exam are as follows:

- Virtual private network (VPN)
- AWS Direct Connect
- Public internet

Figure 3.3 diagrams mental models of the ways you can connect to cloud computing resources with your local devices while utilizing a VPN and the public internet.

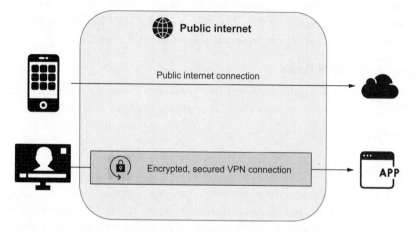

Figure 3.3   There are different ways your local devices can connect to the AWS Cloud. Two examples are the public internet and VPNs.

When you first create an AWS account, you find that AWS creates an *Amazon Virtual Private Cloud* (Amazon VPC) for you. Amazon VPC is a private, isolated corner of AWS, where you can begin building your IT infrastructure. Consider that your home Wi-Fi network is a private network where you can house your devices, like a printer, tablet, computer, and phone, and the network is isolated from everyone else's Wi-Fi network. AWS VPC is a virtual network that is also isolated from other virtual networks so that other customers don't have access to your IT infrastructure housed in Amazon VPC.

Because Amazon VPC is a virtual network housed in AWS, you must be able to connect to it from your local computer or server. Let's find out what some of these connectivity options are!

VIRTUAL PRIVATE NETWORK

While AWS does offer a service called AWS VPN, the concept of a VPN is not original to AWS. The technology dates back to the mid-1990s, when a Microsoft employee created a "peer-to-peer tunneling protocol" that helped to pave the way for a more secure connection between a local device and the internet.

A VPN provides privacy and security online by creating an encrypted private network between your device and the resource you are connecting to, even when you are utilizing a public internet connection. VPNs hide your IP address, which means that who you are and what you are doing becomes harder for snoopers to trace. You might have some friends who use VPNs to connect to streaming websites that are region-blocked to watch their favorite movies or TV shows not available in their own countries. This can happen because the VPN service they are utilizing hides their real location from the streaming servers.

AWS is one of countless VPN services available. Its VPN service is called *AWS Virtual Private Network* and consists of AWS Client VPN and AWS Site-to-Site VPN. AWS VPN creates secure connections between your on-premises networks and AWS's global network.

AWS Client VPN allows your remote workers to securely connect to resources in the AWS Cloud and your *on-premises networks* (network in your office or data center). *AWS Site-to-Site VPN* enables you to create secured connections between different locations (like your multiple offices and data centers) and the AWS Cloud. The distinction seems a bit murky, especially if these terms are new. However, for the purposes of this book, which is to expose you to different concepts assuming you don't need to turn around and configure them, you might think of the difference between AWS Client VPN and AWS Site-to-Site VPN like this: Client VPN utilizes single-user connections (for example, a laptop to a certain network), while Site-to-Site VPNs connect entire networks together (for example, office network with another office network). Whichever VPN tool you end up utilizing, accessing the AWS Cloud using a VPN allows you to establish a more secure and private connection between your local devices or offices and your AWS Cloud infrastructure.

AWS DIRECT CONNECT

AWS Direct Connect is an AWS service that connects your local network directly to the AWS Cloud. It creates a secure, private connection between your local network and AWS, which means that it bypasses the public internet. Having your local network directly connected to your AWS infrastructure gives you more predictable and low-latency network performance and reduces bandwidth costs. Figure 3.4 shows how AWS Direct Connect creates a direct connection between your local network and the AWS Cloud, which can reduce bandwidth costs and provide more reliable and faster network performance.

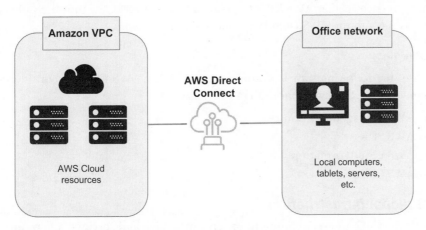

Figure 3.4   AWS Direct Connect creates a direct connection between your local network and the AWS Cloud.

This way of connecting to the AWS Cloud infrastructure may be a great way to build a hybrid deployment infrastructure, as it allows you to connect your on-premises networks (and by extension, your on-premises IT resources) with the AWS Cloud without compromising performance. Because AWS Direct Connect is considered the "shortest path" between your local network and the AWS Cloud, it may also be useful for managing large data transfers like rapid data backup, broadcast media processing, or real-time data analysis.

PUBLIC INTERNET

According to the American Heritage Dictionary of the English Language, the *public internet* is a "publicly accessible system of networks that connects computers around the world via the TCP/IP protocol." If you are scrolling on your smartphone using mobile data from a wireless carrier to check the latest gossip articles, you are likely using the public internet.

We don't need to get too deep into what the TCP/IP is, but in short, it is an abbreviation of *transmission control protocol/internet protocol*, which is a set of rules allowing communication between computers on a network. The most well-known network utilizing the TCP/IP is the public internet.

Unlike utilizing AWS VPN or AWS Direct Connect, the public internet is not secure or private. Your data is not encrypted during transit, and you cannot hide who you are or what you are doing. People or organizations with malicious intent could pick up what you are doing, what you are typing, and the conversations you have online without much trouble when you utilize the public internet to communicate.

While utilizing the public internet for casual browsing and social media use may be acceptable, if you are working on IT infrastructure housed on the AWS Cloud, taking advantage of a more private and secure network is probably the better option to keep your data and resources secured. If you do need to use the public internet, you can rely on a service such as AWS VPN to create a private network within the public internet to connect to the AWS Cloud on a more secure network.

3.2.4   *Section quiz*

Which of the following ways to communicate with the AWS Cloud is considered programmatic? (There may be more than one answer.)

    a AWS Management Console
    b AWS SDKs
    c AWS CloudFormation
    d AWS Chime

3.3   *AWS global infrastructure*

With its presence in every continent except Antarctica and serving 245 countries and territories, Amazon's infrastructure is truly global. As of 2022, the AWS Cloud spans 81 Availability Zones (AZs) and 25 Regions, with 27 more AZs and 9 more Regions in the works. AWS boasts two times more Regions with multiple AZs than the next largest cloud computing platform. With millions of active customers across virtually every industry, it has the largest and most dynamic cloud ecosystem in the world.

Having such a global footprint allows AWS to provide security, availability, performance, scalability, and flexibility to its customers. A big part of understanding how the AWS global infrastructure operates is learning about the relationships between *AWS Regions*, *AZs*, and *Edge Locations*.

3.3.1 Regions

AWS Regions are physical locations around the globe where AWS clusters data centers called Availability Zones. Each Region has two or more AZs, serving customers in the physical areas around them. As of the beginning of 2022, AWS had 25 geographic Regions, with plans for 9 more coming to previously underserved areas of the world.

When creating an AWS infrastructure, you should choose to house it in the Region and AZ physically closest to you to get the highest performance possible. One thing to keep in mind is that not all Regions or AZs are made equal, and some services are available only in certain Regions or AZs. AWS's general policy is that it will make new services and features available to all AWS Regions within 12 months of general availability when possible.

Each Region is completely isolated from the others so that if one Region goes down due to a human-made or natural disaster, the other Regions remain unaffected. Designing each Region to be completely isolated provides the greatest possible fault tolerance and stability for your IT infrastructure.

UTILIZING MULTIPLE AWS REGIONS

With the understanding that each AWS Region is completely isolated from every other Region, your company may opt to utilize multiple AWS Regions, often replicating the data hosted in one Region to another. Replicating data in multiple Regions may help with business continuity or data recovery, because when one Region loses data or has an outage, you can immediately jump over to your other Regions to maintain business continuity. This concept is called *fault tolerance.*

Fault tolerance is the ability of a system to stay operational even if parts of the system fail. In this case, even if one Region fails, because the resources and data are replicated in one or more other Regions, your business can remain operational. As an added bonus, when your resources are replicated in multiple Regions, when one Region fails and the data is lost, there are multiple copies of the same data in other unaffected Regions. While fault tolerance is great for keeping your infrastructure up and running despite bumps and jolts that come with the real world (and real natural disasters), it can potentially get rather expensive.

Hosting resources in multiple AWS Regions can also provide low latency for end users, as they can access the AWS-hosted resources via data centers in the Region closest to their physical presence. If your online course streaming company's physical presence is in Virginia, USA, and you host your resources in the US East Region

(Region name: N. Virginia; Region: us-east-1), your customers from Seoul, South Korea may have latency issues when trying to stream your videos. By having replicated data in the Asia Pacific Region (Region name: Seoul; Region: ap-northeast-2), you can make sure your customers in Asia Pacific can enjoy the same user experience that your US customers do.

Different countries and territories have different regulations and laws when it comes to storing data, which is referred to as *data sovereignty*. AWS has powerful tools that allow you to control where your data is stored, how it is secured, and who can access it. When you utilize AWS services, you can remain confident that your data stays within the AWS Region that you selected to house the resources. Utilizing multiple AWS Regions allows you to control where every piece of your data is stored to stay within regulations in each of the territories and countries in which your company operates.

3.3.2   *Availability Zones*

Each AWS Region has two or more AZs, which are discrete data centers with redundant power, networking, and connectivity. Each AZ may have one or more data centers, and all AZs in a single Region are interconnected with high-bandwidth, low-latency networking.

In layperson's terms, this means that the data transfer speed between AZs in a single Region is lightning fast. AWS states that each AZ is physically separate from other AZs in the same AWS Region by a meaningful distance, but they are within 60 miles of each other. What does that mean for the roundtrip latency of data? It's usually within a few milliseconds! That's superfast!

Figure 3.5 diagrams how AWS Regions are distinct physical locations around the world with two or more AZs. AZs are logical data centers that provide low latency and high availability for AWS customers.

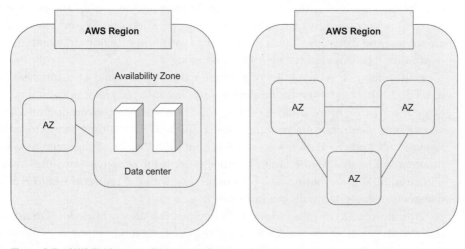

Figure 3.5   AWS Regions are distinct physical locations around the world with two or more AZs. AZs are logical data centers.

You generally choose the AZ that is closest to your physical location, similarly to Regions. You can also utilize multiple AZs (in multiple Regions, if you choose) to make your resources more highly available, resilient, and accessible to customers everywhere.

UTILIZING MULTIPLE AVAILABILITY ZONES

All AZs, even within a single Region, are separated by a meaningful distance (but they reside within 60 miles of each other), which means that when natural disasters such as earthquakes, tornadoes, or lightning strikes bring one AZ down, other AZs in the same Region can take over or continue operations. When you host or replicate your resources in multiple AZs, no single AZ becomes a single point of failure because each AZ has its own power, networking, and connectivity, as well as servers (they are data centers, after all!). Utilizing multiple AZs allows your AWS Cloud resources to achieve high availability. You can design your AWS Cloud infrastructure to fail over automatically between AZs to avoid interruptions when one malfunctions or goes down. Utilizing multiple AZs to host your resources allows you to achieve highly available, fault-tolerant, and scalable IT infrastructure in the AWS Cloud.

> ### Fault tolerance vs. high availability
> What's the difference? A little confusing? I totally get it!
>
> Achieving high availability requires replicating resources within AZs within the *same* Region. It is less costly than achieving fault tolerance, which requires replication in *multiple* Regions.
>
> Fault-tolerant infrastructures are, by nature, highly available (as they also replicate resources within each Region), but highly available infrastructures are not necessarily fault tolerant (unless they are also replicating to multiple Regions).

3.3.3 Edge Locations

Edge Locations are physical data centers that Amazon CloudFront uses to cache copies of your data for faster content delivery to users. (We learn about Amazon CloudFront in more detail in a few paragraphs, but in a nutshell, it is an AWS service that speeds up distribution of web content by utilizing caching.) They exist at the closest location to your end users so that there is the lowest latency possible when delivering requested data.

 Data caching refers to the concept of keeping data and files temporarily in a special storage space to make websites, devices, and applications run more efficiently. When you visit your favorite news site, you are likely not reloading every single piece of information, image, and video every time you visit. Your browser keeps a *cache* of data so that only parts (often the updated parts) of the web page are reloaded in subsequent visits. This helps to cut down on loading time (data latency) so you can have a very efficient browsing experience scrolling through all of your cat memes (no judgment).

AWS has Edge Locations to do the same thing your browser does when it visits websites so that its users can download data from the closest point possible. Let's go back to the example of an online video course company physically located in Virginia, USA, with its Region of choice and AZs located in the East Coast of the United States. Without Edge Locations, the video content a customer in Seoul, South Korea wants to watch has to be streamed from data centers halfway across the globe. Thankfully, because Edge Locations physically closest to the customer in Seoul will cache the data once the first person downloads it (sorry, first person—you had to suffer the long load time), all subsequent users based in that area will be able to stream videos directly from the closest Edge Location, improving their user experience.

AMAZON CLOUDFRONT

What powers all of this caching is *Amazon CloudFront,* an AWS service that speeds up the distribution of static and dynamic web content by caching the content at Edge Locations. Amazon CloudFront identifies where the request for data is coming from and routes the distribution through the AWS network to find the Edge Location that can most efficiently serve the content to the end user. Not only does Amazon CloudFront help with delivering content with lower latency, but it also helps to increase the reliability and availability of your data because copies of your files are now cached in multiple Edge Locations around the world. Win–win!

AWS GLOBAL ACCELERATOR

Another way to improve performance for local and global users utilizing Edge Locations is to take advantage of the *AWS Global Accelerator.* AWS Global Accelerator directs traffic over the AWS global network to endpoints in the nearest Region to the customer. What it actually does is a little difficult to grasp in words, so let's take a look at figure 3.6.

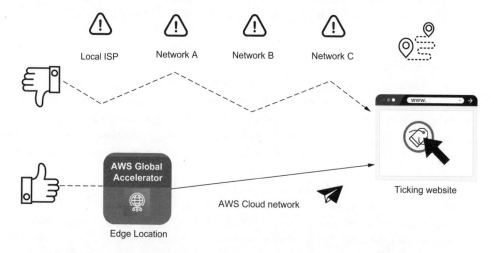

Figure 3.6 AWS Global Accelerator allows website owners to help users access their websites and web applications faster and more efficiently by maximizing the amount of time the web traffic spends in the superfast AWS network.

In figure 3.6, the thumbs-down icon symbolizes users accessing a ticketing website without AWS Global Accelerator. When a highly coveted ticket to see a famous musician is released, users' requests are routed through many different networks before they reach the data centers housing the ticketing web application. The data the requests bring back from the web application goes through similar delays. Every new network the user's request hits results in latency, or lag.

In contrast, the AWS Global Accelerator speeds up the content delivery process by utilizing Edge Locations and the AWS network. By routing each request to the user's closest Edge Location, AWS Global Accelerator throws the requests onto the high-speed, congestion-free AWS global network. When the ticketing website's owner enables AWS Global Accelerator, users trying to grab a ticket can get on the "internet freeway" and make their purchases efficiently. By maximizing the amount of time the web traffic is on the AWS network as opposed to the public network, this service accelerates the content delivery speed.

You can imagine the regular requests as using local roads and highways during rush hour, while AWS Global Accelerator is like having the ability to take a toll road and bypass the heavy traffic. By maximizing the amount of time you are driving on the toll road rather than the traffic-laden local roads, you speed up your commute substantially. In the case of AWS Global Accelerator, the availability and performance of data delivery can go up by 60%!

3.3.4   Section quiz

To achieve high availability, you should utilize multiple _____.

a   Edge Locations

b   AZs

c   Regions

d   Wavelength Zones

Summary

- Two large infrastructure concepts that pertain to hosting your IT infrastructure in AWS are deploying and operating in AWS and the AWS global infrastructure.
- There are many ways to interact with the AWS Cloud. Some are programmatic, and others are graphical. All interactions with the AWS Cloud utilize APIs.
- Some ways to interact with AWS that you should keep in mind are the AWS Management Console, AWS CLI, AWS SDKs, and AWS IaC.
- The three ways of deploying IT infrastructure in the AWS Cloud are cloud/cloud native, hybrid, and on-premises.
- Some connectivity options in the AWS Cloud are VPN, AWS Direct Connect, and the public internet.
- AWS Regions are physically isolated locations around the world with two or more logical data centers, which are called Availability Zones.

- Edge Locations are data centers that cache data and help transport data as quickly as possible to the consumer. An Edge Location is the closest in physical distance to the consumer.
- Amazon CloudFront and AWS Global Accelerator are two services that utilize Edge Locations to speed up content delivery.

Chapter quiz answers

- 3.2.4: b, c.
  - *Answer*—There are numerous ways for you to communicate programmatically with the AWS Cloud, which allows you to invoke actions through a third-party tool or program. Of the four options in question 3.2.4, AWS SDKs and AWS CloudFormation are the two ways to programmatically access AWS.
- 3.3.4: b.
  - *Answer*—To achieve high availability with your AWS Cloud infrastructure, you should utilize multiple AZs.

Core AWS services

This chapter covers

- Introducing core compute services
- Identifying core storage services
- Reviewing core database services
- Evaluating networking and content delivery services
- Examining AWS management tools

In chapter 3, we learned about hosting IT infrastructure on AWS, methods of deploying and operating in AWS, and how the AWS global infrastructure works to provide secure and reliable cloud computing services. In this chapter, we continue learning about different parts of the AWS Cloud by identifying core compute, storage, database, networking, and content delivery services and the different AWS management tools available.

4.1 Compute services

Some of the most widely used AWS services are its compute services. As the name suggests, AWS's compute services provides cloud-based computational resources to its customers. Previously, to acquire computing power, you had to physically purchase a computer or server with technical specifications that matched your needs.

This process was both costly and time-consuming because purchasing a physical machine required upfront capital, and the procurement process could take weeks, if not months. You had to choose the appropriate machine, get it approved by the bosses/finance/management, make the order, and receive the order. Now, thanks to cloud computing's pay-as-you-go model, you only pay for what you use without long-term contracts or complex licensing that bloats costs in legacy IT infrastructure.

There are a few different categories of AWS compute services. The categories help you to quickly identify their purposes such as virtual machines versus cost and capacity management. They are as follows:

- *Instances (virtual machines)*—Amazon Elastic Compute Cloud (Amazon EC2), Amazon Lightsail
- *Containers*—Amazon Elastic Container Service (Amazon ECS), Amazon Fargate
- *Serverless*—AWS Lambda
- *Edge and hybrid*—AWS Outposts, AWS Wavelength
- *Cost and capacity management*—AWS Elastic Beanstalk, Elastic Load Balancing (ELB)

These categories of AWS compute services allow users to achieve a variety of computational goals ranging from deploying a secure virtual machine (a server running on cloud computing) in the cloud with Amazon EC2 to running code without worrying about maintaining servers with AWS Lambda.

In this section, we examine the following core AWS compute services:

- Amazon EC2
- AWS Elastic Beanstalk
- ELB
- AWS Lambda
- Amazon ECS

4.1.1   *Amazon Elastic Compute Cloud*

Amazon Elastic Compute Cloud, more commonly referred to as Amazon EC2 (Get it? Compute Cloud? C2?), is arguably one of the most popular and highly utilized services AWS offers. Amazon EC2 is a scalable cloud computing service that gives you the ability to quickly configure and deploy virtual machines that fit your needs. Each virtual machine you create (sometimes referred to as *spin up*) is called an *instance*, and the different configuration types available for these instances (such as CPU, memory, and storage) are called *instance types*.

You can spin up as many or as few virtual machines as you need, each with granular controls so you can get exactly what you want. Because you are in essence "renting" the compute resources from AWS, you do not have to invest in procuring hardware up front, which saves time, money, and labor.

The usage of Amazon EC2 is billed based on the following:

- Number of hours the instance is being utilized
- Size of the instance
- Region it is deployed in
- Type of operating system it uses

The service integrates very well with other AWS services (such as database services), which makes architecting an IT infrastructure in AWS much easier. For those of you who want to get rolling quickly, AWS offers preconfigured templates for your Amazon EC2 instances called *Amazon Machine Images* (AMIs). AMIs package settings you need to spin up a server, such as operating systems and software, so that you can configure and deploy a virtual machine in just minutes. If you are so inclined, you can even create your own AMIs so you can quickly deploy resources with standardized configurations.

One of the most prominent features of Amazon EC2 is its ability to auto scale. *Scaling* is the process in which resources are procured when needs arise, as well as contract, or release, resources when they are no longer necessary. In IT jargon, people refer to these types of flexible changes as "scaling out, scaling in" or "scaling up, scaling down."

An example of a situation where scaling may be necessary is before a big annual sale for an online shop. You may be expecting 10 or even 100 times the regular visitor traffic and purchases on your e-commerce website. With legacy IT infrastructure, you would have to purchase servers with this huge surge in mind. While purchasing the buffed-up servers for this one event may help to prevent system overwhelm during the one-week sale, the resources are wasted for the remainder of the year when the customer traffic is just a fraction of that during the sale period.

Scaling up (increasing the resources to meet the surge in demand when the sale occurs) and then scaling back down (decreasing the resources when the sale is over so that resources and money are not wasted) allows a company to save money and time as it navigates fluxes in demand. Amazon EC2 makes this process even smoother by helping achieve *elasticity* through auto scaling.

Elasticity and auto scaling allow your IT resources to automatically acquire resources as you need them and release them when they are no longer necessary. You can imagine a rubber band stretching automatically when there's pressure to extend and then contracting back down when the pressure is no longer there. Rubber bands can expand and contract because of elasticity, and auto-scaling IT resources work the same way. Elasticity is part of the performance efficiency pillar of the AWS's Well-Architected Framework we learned about in chapter 2.

4.1.2   *AWS Elastic Beanstalk*

Plant a seed and watch the beanstalk grow! AWS Elastic Beanstalk is a compute service that helps you upload your application code into the service (the seed); it automatically springs up the web application on AWS for you (the beanstalk), taking care of details such as resource provisioning, load balancing, auto scaling, and monitoring.

OK, so I'm reaching a little with the analogy, but I hope you get my drift. Not only does it deploy the web application for you automatically, but it also tracks and monitors your web application's health. It can also auto scale your application in and out based on changing requirements. For developers, this service can definitely seem like a magic bean(stalk)!

Figure 4.1 shows how AWS Elastic Beanstalk takes your web application's code and spins up the web application for you, utilizing different AWS services such as Load Balancer, Amazon EC2, and Amazon Simple Storage Service (Amazon S3).

To utilize AWS Elastic Beanstalk, ideally you write the web application code in PHP, Java, Python, Ruby, Node.js, .Net, or Go or use a container service called Docker. Once you upload the code into AWS Elastic Beanstalk, AWS utilizes different AWS services, such as Amazon EC2 and ELB, to deploy the web application to the cloud for you. You can deploy your code through the AWS Management Console, Elastic Beanstalk command-line interface, Visual Studio, and Eclipse. You also have the option

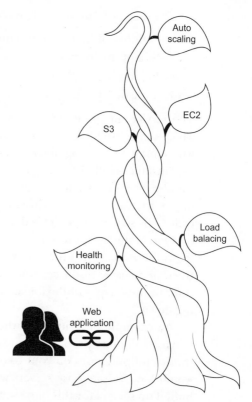

Figure 4.1   AWS Elastic Beanstalk helps developers focus on coding by taking care of the deployment, auto scaling, and health monitoring of the application for them.

of controlling which AWS resources you want to use to power your web application (such as the instance type for Amazon EC2) and can take over any or all of the management of your IT infrastructure at any time.

Great news! AWS Elastic Beanstalk is free to use. You only pay for the resources you are using (such as Amazon EC2 instances or Amazon S3 storage) when you are building and managing your infrastructure with AWS Elastic Beanstalk but not for the privilege of using the service itself.

4.1.3   *Elastic Load Balancing*

Elastic Load Balancing, or ELB, automatically redistributes incoming web application traffic across multiple *targets*, or compute resources, such as Amazon EC2 instances, to help your web application increase availability. It also monitors the health of your targets (in this case, Amazon EC2 instances) to make sure it only routes traffic to healthy instances. This feature also allows you to add compute resources from or remove them from the load balancers without disrupting the overall flow of traffic to your applications because ELB automatically reroutes the requests based on the changes.

ELB can also scale your load balancer up or down as traffic changes over time, such as with the annual sale example we reviewed when learning about Amazon EC2's auto-scaling capabilities. Amazon EC2 can automatically scale your compute resources up or down depending on fluctuations in need, and ELB can automatically balance the incoming traffic loads so the influx of web traffic does not flood one server and take it down.

There are currently four different types of load balancers:

- Application load balancer
- Network load balancer
- Gateway load balancer
- Classic load balancer

Each type of load balancer has specific strengths. For example, an application load balancer is great for flexible application management, while extreme performance needs may work better with a network load balancer. As a cloud architect, you pick the type of load balancer that most closely matches your needs to balance your web traffic toward your compute resources.

NOTE Interested in learning more about the different types of load balancers? Check out the developer guide for load balancer types here: http://mng .bz/rnax.

Some of the different services that ELB can work with are Amazon EC2, AWS Certificate Manager, AWS Global Accelerator, and Amazon CloudWatch, among others. With any partnership it has, ELB can improve the availability and scalability of your applications. Like Amazon EC2, you pay for what you use. The billing is calculated based on the number of load-balancer units being utilized per hour and for each hour (or partial hour) of use.

4.1.4 *AWS Lambda*

Serverless services allow you to run code without the need to launch and maintain servers. While the name is a little misleading—because even though it's "serverless" to you, you are running your code on someone's servers (in this case, AWS's servers in its data centers)—utilizing these services relieves you from spinning up, patching, or otherwise maintaining your own servers.

You might compare it to borrowing a rental kitchen to record your YouTube cooking show. All the equipment is there for you, clean and prepped, and you simply need to show up with the ingredients (code) and cook (run the code). Currently, there are a little over two dozen compute services in this specific service group.

Want to run code but don't want to deal with the overhead tasks and responsibilities related to configuring and managing servers? AWS Lambda is the serverless compute service for you! It is an event-driven compute service, which allows you to "trigger" Lambda functions to run code for virtually any type of application or service. Lambda functions are resources you can call on to run your code in AWS Lambda.

You can think of lambda functions like recipes that you invoke when a restaurant customer orders a specific meal. The recipe is dormant in your mind until the order is put in, at which time you, as the cook, can spring into action, utilizing different resources (ingredients) in the kitchen to whip up the delicious meal. You can trigger AWS Lambda from over 200 AWS services and applications, which makes it a cost-effective way to design your web application infrastructure.

Figure 4.2 shows an example workflow using AWS Lambda, where you utilize image processing to resize images upon upload. A user may upload a profile photo for a social media application, which is uploaded to Amazon S3, a storage service. That action is set to trigger AWS Lambda to begin processing the images by running code to resize the images for different browser sizes (a lambda function).

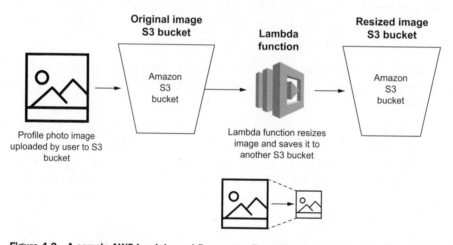

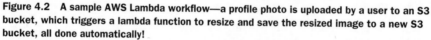

Figure 4.2   A sample AWS Lambda workflow—a profile photo is uploaded by a user to an S3 bucket, which triggers a lambda function to resize and save the resized image to a new S3 bucket, all done automatically!

You only need the code "waiting" for the trigger (a new image uploaded by the user) for it to complete its task instead of worrying about managing the backend infrastructure. AWS Lambda can also automatically scale based on demand, so even if it gets an influx of new users trying to upload new profile photos at the same time, it can process all of the requests in real time.

You could spin up a virtual machine on Amazon EC2, pay for that, and spend some time configuring and managing the virtual machine to run your code. Or, you can save money, time, and human resources by paying only for the compute time you use while the lambda function is running by utilizing AWS Lambda!

4.1.5 *Amazon Elastic Container Service*

So far, we have learned about Amazon EC2, which belongs to the *instance* type of compute services. We have also learned about ELB and AWS Elastic Beanstalk, which are categorized as *cost and capacity management* services. AWS Lambda is a serverless type of compute service. Now, we come to Amazon Elastic Container Service, or Amazon ECS, which, as you might have guessed from the name, belongs in the *container* category of compute services.

First, we need to review what containers are. Containers provide a lightweight and consistent way for developers to package and deploy applications. Developers can package an application's code, configurations, and dependencies into a single object (container), creating an isolation of processes. Basically, containers allow developers to create packages (think of a container like a cardboard box) where they have everything they need "inside" to deploy an application. Having all the parts (like code) and configurations prepackaged means that the developer can just pick it up and deploy it in different environments.

Amazon ECS is a fully managed container orchestration service that helps developers launch thousands of these containers on the AWS Cloud. Previously, you needed to install and operate your own container orchestration software, but with a fully managed container orchestration service, you can easily run and scale containerized applications, saving developers time, money, and labor.

And like AWS Elastic Beanstalk, it's free to use! You just pay for the resources you use (like AWS Fargate) when deploying with Amazon ECS, but there is no charge for the using the service itself.

4.1.6 *Section quiz*

Which of the following core AWS compute services helps to balance incoming traffic to different resources (like virtual servers) so that a single resource does not get overwhelmed and go down?

- a   AWS Lambda
- b   Amazon Elastic Container Service
- c   Elastic Load Balancing
- d   AWS Elastic Beanstalk

4.2 *Storage services*

Along with core compute services, storage services are some of the most popular and widely used services in AWS. *Storage services*, as the name suggests, help you store data in AWS.

AWS offers storage for three types of data:

- Object storage
- File storage
- Block storage

Let's take a moment to look at figure 4.3 to visualize the different types of cloud data storage and compare them to types of storage we may be more familiar with on a daily basis.

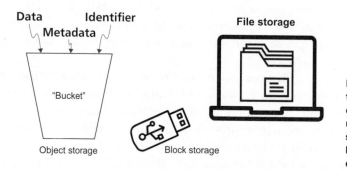

Data   **Identifier**

Metadata

"Bucket"

Object storage

Block storage

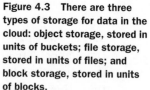

File storage

Figure 4.3   There are three types of storage for data in the cloud: object storage, stored in units of buckets; file storage, stored in units of files; and block storage, stored in units of blocks.

Object storage may be the most difficult type of cloud storage to visualize. Files are broken down into pieces called *objects*, which are placed in buckets. Your real-life buckets may store dirt for gardening, while these cloud buckets store data pieces (objects). Object storage allows you to store massive amounts of unstructured data. You store objects such as photos or videos in Google Photos using object storage. Each object has three components: the data itself, metadata (additional descriptive properties that help with indexing and management of data), and the identifier (address given to the unit of data so it can be located within the hard drive).

Object storage is best suited for *static data*—data that doesn't dynamically change or evolve—because objects can't be modified once placed there. Because object storage utilizes a flat structure, you can scale to huge quantities of data. And thanks to the identifiers and metadata embedded in each object, you or your application can find the data quickly regardless of how much data exists within the infrastructure. Amazon S3 is an example of an AWS service that utilizes object storage.

File storage, on the other hand, is a lot easier to conceptualize: data is stored as pieces of information inside a folder, like files within a folder on your laptop. Unlike object storage, file storage has a hierarchy, and folders can be inside other folders. You must know the exact location of the piece of data you are looking for to find it, which can be a long search if the piece of data is housed a few folders down the logical hierarchy. This is the file storage type we are most familiar with as we've been using it for decades when we store or access files in folders on our desktop computers. Amazon Elastic File System (Amazon EFS) is an example of an AWS service utilizing file storage.

Block storage stores data in units called *blocks*. Like object storage, block storage stores unique identifiers to each block so it can be retrieved from wherever it's being stored. Blocks of data are distributed among multiple environments, and when the data is requested, the blocks are reassembled for the user. Generally, the system utilizes storage-area network environments, managed by a server.

In our daily lives, we utilize a similar concept to block storage when we use USB thumb or external hard drives. We save data onto these devices and can then connect these blocks of storage to whatever computer we wish to access everything we saved on them. Amazon Elastic Block Store (Amazon EBS) is an example of an AWS service utilizing block storage.

The core storage services we learn about in the next section are as follows:

- Amazon S3
- Amazon EBS
- AWS Snowball
- AWS Storage Gateway
- Amazon EFS

4.2.1   *Amazon Simple Storage Service*

Amazon Simple Storage Service, or Amazon S3, is one of the most widely utilized AWS services available. It is an object storage service that allows you to store a virtually limitless amount of data for a wide variety of use cases and offers scalability, data availability, security, and performance. As with many other core AWS services, Amazon S3 partners well with other AWS services, allowing you to create a customized IT infrastructure to suit your needs. Because it is an object storage service, you store data (objects) in buckets. Each object can be up to 5 TB (a terabyte is 1000 GB, which is 1000 MB—so pretty huge)!

Amazon S3 has different storage classes for different needs and budgets, which makes it an attractive choice for companies and people looking to store their data in AWS while being cognizant of their budgets. Each class is built for specific use cases, as well as how often the data needs to be accessed.

Currently, the available Amazon S3 storage classes are as follows:

- S3 Intelligent-Tiering
- S3 Standard
- S3 Standard-Infrequent Access
- S3 One Zone-Infrequent Access
- S3 Glacier Instant Retrieval
- S3 Glacier Flexible Retrieval
- S3 Glacier Deep Archive
- S3 Outposts

Amazon S3 also provides S3 Lifecycle configurations that help you configure how data is migrated from one storage class to another depending on the importance of data, time, or how often the data needs to be retrieved. Moving from one storage class to a lower-cost storage class can save money, while the S3 Lifecycle policies automatically make the transition for you based on predetermined triggers that save you time and labor.

AMAZON S3 GLACIER

The different storage classes for Amazon S3 provide users with various price points for different uses and access frequencies. While storage classes such as Amazon S3 Standard are used for data that may require rather frequent access, the Amazon S3 Glacier series of classes are positioned to store data for longer periods. Amazon S3 Glacier provides extremely low-cost, secure, and highly durable data storage, often utilized for data archiving and backup. For cost-effective long-term storage, you can use the Amazon S3 Glacier classes, such as S3 Glacier Flexible Retrieval, instead of the higher priced but potentially more easily accessible classes of S3 storage.

4.2.2 *Amazon Elastic Block Store*

Amazon Elastic Block Store, or Amazon EBS, as the name suggests, is a block storage service that provides block-level storage volumes to use with Amazon EC2 instances. Conceptually, it is similar to how you use an external hard drive (Amazon EBS) with your desktop computer (Amazon EC2).

While Amazon EBS is utilized with Amazon EC2 instances, it can exist on its own without being attached to EC2 instances. EBS volumes behave like raw, unformatted block devices and are chameleons of sorts. You can utilize Amazon EBS in a variety of ways such as creating a file system on top of these volumes or simply as a block device (think: external hard drives). Each Amazon EC2 virtual machine is called an *instance*, and its equivalent in Amazon EBS is called a *volume*.

Amazon EBS has different volume types similar to storage class types for Amazon S3. Each type of volume has a different use case based on performance characteristics and price.

The Amazon EBS volume types are as follows:

- *Solid state drives* (SSD)—General Purpose SSD, Provisioned IOPS SSD
- *Hard disk drives* (HDD)—Throughput Optimized HDD, Cold HDD
- *Previous generation*—Magnetic

For the purpose of this book, you don't need to know exactly what these types mean, but it's important to note that, like Amazon S3 storage classes, different volume types have different use cases, cost-effectiveness, and performance characteristics. If you are considering utilizing Amazon EBS, you need to research the characteristics and price points of each option before committing.

> **NOTE** If you'd like to dive deeper into the different Amazon EBS volume types, you can take a look here: https://aws.amazon.com/ebs/volume-types/.

4.2.3 *AWS Snowball*

The AWS Snow Family is a collection of physical portable devices that allow you to collect and process data as edge infrastructure as well as migrate (enormous amounts of) data into and out of AWS. The AWS Snow family currently consists of AWS Snowcone, AWS Snowball, and AWS Snowmobile.

To utilize devices in the AWS Snow family as a data transfer service, you receive the physical device in the mail (or in the case of AWS Snowmobile, an actual truck comes to you). You then transfer the data directly to the device and mail it back for efficient upload to the AWS Cloud.

You may recall that AWS's Edge Locations are the closest point to the user, designed to deliver services with the lowest possible latency (delay between request and response). Edge infrastructure provides users the ability to take advantage of cloud computing technology but are closer to the user. AWS's Snow family does this by providing physical storage devices that allow customers to process data in non–data center environments and locations with inconsistent network connectivity. These devices can be thought of as "AWS on the go," providing compute and storage capabilities.

While AWS Snowmobile, a truck pulling a 45-foot-long ruggedized shipping container that can move up to 100 PB of data, is a data migration service, AWS Snowcone and AWS Snowball can also serve as data migration, storage, and compute services. AWS Snowcone is the smallest member of the family, providing edge computing and data transfer at mere 4.5 lbs.

AWS Snowball, on the other hand, weighs in at almost 50 lbs, but packs a punch in terms of compute and storage capacities. There are two types of AWS Snowball devices: Compute Optimize and Storage Optimized. AWS Snowball Edge Compute Optimized provides 42 TB of HDD storage and 208 GB of memory, whereas AWS Snowball Edge Storage Optimized provides 80 TB of HDD storage and 80 GB of memory.

Imagine you are an ornithologist (zoologist who studies birds) researching a new breed of bird you discovered on your last trip to the Amazon rainforest. You have a lot of data and need a durable yet high-capacity computing and storage device to crunch all sorts of data. You might rent an AWS Snowball to utilize as a compute, storage, and edge infrastructure for your months-long trip away from stable internet connectivity. Once you're back home, you can ship the AWS Snowball back to AWS to have the gigabytes of data efficiently uploaded into the cloud. Then, you can utilize other AWS services to further analyze your data. Hopefully you've made an important discovery worthy of publication! As with other AWS services, you choose the AWS Snow family member based on your computational and storage needs as well as your budget.

4.2.4 AWS Storage Gateway

Even when the decision is made to migrate a company's entire IT infrastructure to a cloud computing platform such as AWS Cloud, the process isn't immediate and will likely take months, if not years. While the transition is in process, the company may have some data in the cloud and other data on-premises. Or the company may decide to upload data backups to the cloud but keep frequently accessed data locally available on-site to reduce latency.

Whatever the use case may be, AWS Storage Gateway can connect on-premises IT infrastructure with cloud-based storage infrastructure, allowing your company to utilize the benefits of cloud computing while retaining data on-site. You can visualize the

AWS Storage Gateway as "sitting" between the AWS Cloud's storage infrastructure and your local on-premises IT infrastructure as a "gate," helping both sides access data securely and efficiently. Figure 4.4 shows how AWS Storage Gateway works as a gate between on-premises IT resources and the AWS Cloud by utilizing the internet so that clients can use both forms of IT infrastructure.

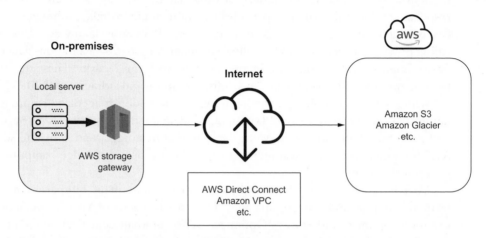

Figure 4.4   AWS Storage Gateway works as a gate between on-premises resources and the AWS Cloud so clients can use both forms of IT infrastructure.

AWS Storage Gateway provides three types of storage gateway solutions:

- *File gateways*—Amazon S3 File Gateway, Amazon FSx File Gateway
- *Volume gateways*—Cached volumes, stored volumes
- *Tape gateways*

Depending on the type of storage gateway solution you choose, you can pick where the data, as well as the cached data, resides. For example, with the Cached Volume Gateway, the data is stored in Amazon S3, but a copy (cache) of frequently accessed data is stored locally for quick and easy access. On the other hand, the Stored Volume Gateway retains the data locally but asynchronously backs up snapshots of the data to Amazon S3. With these two types of volume gateways, the location of the actual data varies, but both work to support durability of data, facilitate partnerships between your on-premises and cloud infrastructure, and save you money.

> **NOTE** Interested in learning more about the different gateway types? Check out this documentation from AWS: https://aws.amazon.com/storagegateway/features/.

As with the previous few storage services, the different types of storage gateway solutions provide different functionalities, access frequency, and price points to meet your specific needs.

4.2.5   *Amazon Elastic File System*

Amazon Elastic File System, or Amazon EFS, is an auto-scaling (elastic) file system that can automatically scale up or down on demand, without disrupting applications. It manages all the file storage infrastructure and provides a simple web interface that allows you to configure file systems quickly and efficiently. It can be used with resources on-premises and with data on the AWS Cloud.

Like Amazon S3, there are different storage classes such as EFS Standard, EFS Standard-Infrequent Access, and EFS One Zone. You select the storage class designed for your storage needs, considering a range of factors such as minimum storage duration, cost, availability, and durability. And, like Amazon S3, Amazon EFS provides life-cycle management so you can save money for files that require archiving.

4.2.6   *Section quiz*

If you are looking for block storage to use with your Amazon EC2 instance, which service would you select?

   a Amazon Elastic File System

   b Amazon Elastic Block Store

   c Amazon Storage Block

   d Amazon S3 Glacier

4.3   *Database services*

Alongside compute and storage services, database services are one of the most well-known and highly utilized services in the AWS Cloud. Professional gamers purchase different types of computers than students who mostly use their computers for writing papers and watching videos. Likewise, different use cases call for different types of databases.

AWS's databases are fully managed, which means that you do not need to be concerned about any backend tasks and labor such as server provisioning, patching, and backups. You just create a database utilizing one of the database services, and you can let AWS manage the rest.

Utilizing database services on AWS tends to be cost-effective, scalable, highly available, and secure. Let's review the core AWS database services that you should become familiar with:

- Amazon Relational Database Service (Amazon RDS)
- Amazon Aurora
- Amazon DynamoDB
- Amazon Redshift

4.3.1   *Amazon Relational Database Service*

Amazon Relational Database Service, or Amazon RDS, is a cloud-based relational database. A *relational database* is a type of database where the types of data stored are related to one another. Amazon RDS is a fully managed database service and is straightforward to set up, operate, and scale.

To visualize what a relational database can look like, let's take a look at figure 4.5. An example of a relational database may be a small business's purchase order process.

Customer ID	Name	Email	Phone Number	Shipping Address
001	Lucy Liu	email@email.com	123-456-7890	Griffith Park Observatory Los Angeles, CA 90068
002	Chris Evans	email@email.com	123-456-7890	Griffith Park Observatory Los Angeles, CA 90068
003	Lupita Nyong'o	email@email.com	123-456-7890	Griffith Park Observatory Los Angeles, CA 90068
004	Rami Malek	email@email.com	123-456-7890	Griffith Park Observatory Los Angeles, CA 90068

Customer ID = "Key"

Customer ID	Order Number	Product Ordered	Quantity
004	0001	Shampoo	2
001	0002	Conditioner	1
001	0003	Soap	4
002	0004	Shampoo	2

Figure 4.5   Relational databases can create a relationship between two (or more) tables by utilizing a unique "key" column.

One table has the unique customer ID (key), name, email, phone number, and shipping address. The second table has the customer ID (the same key), order number, product(s) ordered, and order quantity. When the fulfillment department is looking at the order table, it is unable to see certain information, such as the customer's name or shipping address.

These two tables are linked because they both utilize the unique ID (key) column. The fulfillment center is able to ship the order once the package is ready by using the customer ID to look up the customer's name and address in the customer information table. This is a relational database in action.

Like Amazon EC2, Amazon RDS is available with several database instance types, depending on your use-case. You can use six different types of database engines to power your Amazon RDS:

- Amazon Aurora
- PostgreSQL
- MySQL
- MariaDB

- Oracle Database
- SQL Server

If you already have a database up and running, you can utilize AWS Database Migration Service to migrate your existing database to Amazon RDS in a snap!

Database engines powering Amazon RDS

We won't be talking about five of the six database engines, as they are types of databases (and you don't need to know how they work to take the AWS Certified Cloud Practitioner exam), but we do learn about Amazon Aurora.

If you're interested in learning more about the different databases and how they work with Amazon RDS, you can take a look at the Amazon RDS knowledge base: http://mng.bz/VylN/.

AMAZON AURORA

Amazon Aurora is a MySQL- and PostgreSQL-compatible relational database with performance and availability rivaling commercial-grade databases but at just one-tenth of the cost! It is fully managed by Amazon RDS, which means you don't have to worry about administrative tasks like hardware maintenance, provisioning, patching, or backups. It is up to five times faster than standard MySQL databases and three times faster than standard PostgreSQL databases.

4.3.2 Amazon DynamoDB

Amazon DynamoDB is a fully managed, serverless, key–value NoSQL database. NoSQL databases store data differently from relational databases and, in general, can be thought of more as a bag filled with data points, rather than organized data as in relational databases. NoSQL databases generally utilize *key–value pairs*, rather than a tabular form, like with relational databases (labeled rows and columns).

Key-value pairs may look like this:

```
{
    "_id" : ObjectID("01010de"),
    "name" : "Sally",
    "email" : "email@email.com"
    "age" : 30
}
```

There is a key ("name") and a value ("Sally") for each pair, and you can quickly search through the whole entire database for information using queries.

Amazon DynamoDB is designed to run petabytes of data, allowing developers to start small and scale as much as they need. As with Amazon RDS, it does not require administrative tasks such as installing software, managing servers, or scaling or adjusting for capacity.

4.3.3   *Amazon Redshift*

Amazon Redshift utilizes SQL to analyze enormous volumes of data across data warehouses, operational databases, and data lakes. Setting up and managing your own data warehouse is expensive and labor-intensive, but Amazon Redshift provides a fully managed data warehouse service to analyze exabytes of data and run complex analytics. Have you heard of the phrase "big data"? Well, Amazon Redshift is definitely meant to crunch that big data!

Data warehouses collect data from a wide range of sources to analyze and run complex reports. The primary function is to run analytics and support business intelligence activities. You can gain up to three times better price performance over other cloud data warehouses at scale, and similar to other database services offered by AWS, you don't have to deal with the administrative aspect of creating and managing databases.

4.3.4   *Section quiz*

Which one of the following databases services does not utilize relational databases?

   a   Amazon Redshift

   b   Amazon RDS

   c   Amazon DynamoDB

4.4   *Networking and content delivery services*

While all the conversations about cool services that help you compute, store, or run databases on the cloud are definitely exciting, none of this would be possible without the networking and content delivery services that bring everything together. Cloud storage is great, but if you don't have a way to access your data on the cloud, you can't utilize it.

The core networking and content delivery services you need foundational knowledge of are as follows:

- Amazon Virtual Private Cloud (section 3.2.3)
- AWS Direct Connect (section 3.2.3)
- Amazon Virtual Private Network (section 3.2.3)
- Amazon CloudFront (section 3.3.3)
- AWS Global Accelerator (section 3.3.3)
- Amazon Route 53

We have already learned about most of the services in chapter 3, so for a refresher, you can head to the section numbers mentioned next to the service names. In this section, we learn about Route 53, which is one of the most important core services to know when beginning your AWS Cloud journey.

4.4.1   Amazon Route 53

Back in the old days, when you wanted to find a mechanic in a new town, you pulled out the Yellow Pages, peered through the index until you found the pages devoted to the town's mechanics, and picked one from the list to call. The Yellow Pages was a telephone directory that listed businesses and other organizations according to the goods or services they offered and was distributed to all residents and businesses within a local coverage area. While the print version is basically obsolete, online versions still persist and are called Internet Yellow Pages.

Why are we talking about the telephone book? Because like the telephone directory that helped you look up who you wanted to call, Amazon Route 53 lets you identify an online resource you want to access and whizzes you to your destination.

Amazon Route 53 is a cloud *domain name system* (DNS). Broken down to its core, a DNS service is the internet's phonebook. When you type in a domain name like `facebook.com` into the address bar of your browser, a DNS service identifies the server you are trying to reach from the sea of servers around the world and takes you to the website. In the backend, DNS services translate URLs like http://facebook.com into numeric IP addresses, which are addresses computers and servers use to connect to each other, and then send you to that specific IP address.

In the Yellow Pages, the names of businesses were listed in an alphabetical order, and when you flipped to the right section based on the name, you found the phone number. Those were the key–value pairs (the key is the name, and the value is the phone number). With a DNS directory, a key–value pair is the business website (such as manning.com), which then calls the "phone number" (the IP of the device or resource).

Figure 4.6 shows a simplified imagery workflow utilizing Amazon Route 53 as a "phone book service for the internet" analogy. When you open a browser and type in a website address URL, such as manning.com, Amazon Route 53 searches through its "phone book directory" of servers and finds the server that hosts Manning Publication's website. Once the server is located, your browser loads the manning.com website so you can browse its content to your heart's desire.

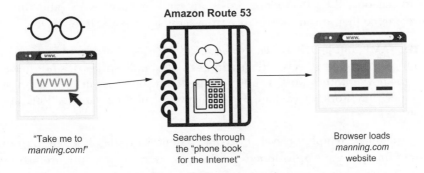

Amazon Route 53

"Take me to *manning.com!*" Searches through the "phone book for the Internet" Browser loads *manning.com* website

Figure 4.6   Amazon Route 53 can be thought of as a "phone book service for the internet," helping you connect to web servers all around the world.

Amazon Route 53 can route users to IT infrastructure running on AWS and can also be used to route users to infrastructure outside of AWS. You can utilize it to help configure failovers, manage traffic globally, and partner with other AWS services to create a highly available, scalable, and secure IT infrastructure. It even offers domain name registration, so you can purchase that dream domain name (yourfavoritecupcake .com) and begin the process of building your own website on AWS!

4.4.2 Section quiz

Amazon Route 53 translates human-readable names such as google.com into _____.

- a Domain name systems
- b IP addresses
- c Domain name registrations
- d Security groups

4.5 Management tools

AWS Management Tools, as the name suggests, allows users to manage their AWS account and components of cloud computing services. These management tools allow you to provision, monitor, and automate the cloud IT infrastructure being housed on the AWS Cloud. Some of the core AWS Management Tools we learn about in this section are as follows:

- AWS CloudFormation
- AWS CloudTrail
- Amazon CloudWatch
- AWS Config
- AWS Trusted Advisor

4.5.1 AWS CloudFormation

AWS CloudFormation is a management tool that speeds up infrastructure provisioning with Infrastructure as Code (if you need a refresher, we learned about Infrastructure as Code in section 3.2.1). It models, provisions, and manages AWS (and third-party) resources by coding your infrastructure from scratch using YAML or JSON.

> **NOTE** YAML and JSON are *data serialization languages* that provide a way for you to present data objects and structures using simple syntax. It's not necessary to know how they work or how to write them yourself, but it's worth noting that they work to exchange data between different applications and languages.

There are many templates available. These templates describe all of the AWS resources that you want provisioned and how you want them configured so that you don't have to directly manage the administrative tasks of getting your application up and running. Having all the configurations defined in code also makes it easy to track changes to your infrastructure, as well as makes replicating certain configurations a breeze.

> **NOTE** If you want to look into AWS CloudFormation templates, you can check out some samples here: http://mng.bz/xMv7.

AWS CloudFormation creates a *stack*—a conceptual structure that makes up an IT infrastructure—based on the template code. As a result, AWS CloudFormation provisions and configures the stacks and resources based on the template, and you end up with an automatically deployed infrastructure that is easily replicable and scalable. With AWS CloudFormation, in just minutes you can whip up anything from a single Amazon EC2 instance to a complex multiregion application using code.

4.5.2 AWS CloudTrail

AWS CloudTrail protects organizations from compliance or regulation violations by tracking user activity and API usage 24/7. Actions taken by users, roles (AWS identity with permission policies that determine what users can and cannot do), or AWS services are recorded as CloudTrail events, and you can easily view recent events in the history log. You can also create a *trail* to follow an ongoing record of activity and events, which may help to identify and react to unusual activity within your account.

You may be alerted to suspicious activity that possibly compromised an Amazon S3 bucket filled with sensitive information, making proprietary information public. It's only a matter of time before a malicious third party finds it and downloads all the information to sell or publish. But thanks to the alerting system you've set up in your AWS infrastructure, you are almost instantaneously alerted to this breach and are able to make the S3 bucket private.

Now, the detective work begins to find out what happened by going through the AWS CloudTrail events log and determining who made the bucket public and when. The AWS CloudTrail events log allows IT and compliance teams to quickly identify and act on security events by giving them quick access to everything that happened leading up to an incident, saving critical time as they piece together information.

Visibility into who is doing what and where is a key component of security and operational best practices. Using AWS CloudTrail, you can search and download account activity, as well as analyze and respond to events.

4.5.3 Amazon CloudWatch

Amazon CloudWatch monitors your resources and applications in AWS in real time. It collects and tracks metrics to enhance observability of your AWS infrastructure so that developers can gain actionable insights and respond to performance changes. It collects monitoring data as logs, metrics, and events, which can be used to detect unusual activities, set alarms, and troubleshoot issues.

Let's go back to the previous example of a data breach where automatic alerting mitigated long-term exposure of sensitive data and the IT and compliance teams utilized

AWS CloudTrail logs to find out who did what to cause it. The initial alerting may have come from an Amazon CloudWatch alarm when it detected this unusual activity. Having automated monitoring provides quick resolutions to otherwise hard-to-identify problems that can have huge business implications.

You can visualize the data on Amazon CloudWatch home page, as well as create custom dashboards to display data about metrics you care about. Amazon CloudWatch collects data for you to analyze to keep your AWS infrastructure running smoothly and efficiently. AWS CloudWatch doesn't charge a minimum fee or require upfront commitments; instead, you pay for what you use.

4.5.4   *AWS Config*

AWS Config is one of those AWS services with a very intuitive name: it literally monitors and manages your AWS config(urations). It continuously monitors and records your AWS resource and service configurations so that you can easily evaluate whether your service configurations match your needs. When you are setting up robust IT infrastructures on AWS, you want to be sure that all services and resources are being set up efficiently, securely, and in compliance with best practices. With AWS Config, you can assess, audit, and evaluate your resource configurations to make sure you're on the right track.

As AWS Config monitors your resource configurations, it can send Amazon Simple Notification Service notifications for you to review or take action on when it notices a configuration update. It automatically sends a configuration history file to an Amazon S3 bucket so you can review the change logs to make sure they are compliant with your specifications and requirements.

With AWS Config, you can to do the following:

- Review configuration changes and relationships between AWS resources.
- Obtain detailed AWS resource configuration histories.
- Determine overall compliance when measured against desired configurations specified in corporate internal guidelines.
- Simplify compliance auditing, security analysis, change management, and operational troubleshooting.

AWS Config isn't free. Charges are based on the number of configuration items recorded, active rule evaluations, and conformance pack evaluations.

4.5.5   *AWS Trusted Advisor*

AWS Trusted Advisor is your trusty IT auditor, walking around your IT infrastructure with a checklist in hand, marking off different ways to optimize your IT infrastructure. This service offers recommendations to get your AWS infrastructure as close as possible to AWS best practices. It does this by using *checks*.

The categories of checks offered by AWS Trusted Advisor are as follows:

- Cost optimization
- Performance
- Security
- Fault tolerance
- Service quotas

Once the checks are run, the service provides recommended actions:

- No problem detected (a check mark)
- Investigation recommended (an exclamation mark in a triangle)
- Action recommended (an exclamation mark in a circle)

Figure 4.7 shows a screenshot of AWS Management Console's AWS Trusted Advisor dashboard with its sample of checks and recommended actions represented by a checkmark, an exclamation mark in a triangle, or an exclamation mark in a circle. When the number of recommended actions is zero, the icons are grayed out.

Figure 4.7   Screenshot of a sample AWS Trusted Advisor dashboard showing the five categories of checks and ways you can potentially optimize your AWS infrastructure

The breadth of types of checks available depends on the support plan in which your AWS account is enrolled, which we learn more about in chapter 6:

- *AWS Basic and AWS Developer support plans*—Core security checks, all checks for service quotas
- *AWS Business and AWS Enterprise support plans*—All checks including cost optimization, security, fault tolerance, performance, and service quotas

4.5.6   *Section quiz*

Which of the following AWS services utilizes Infrastructure as Code?

a   AWS Trusted Advisor

b   Amazon CloudWatch

c   Amazon CloudTrail

d   AWS CloudFormation

Summary

- Compute services provide cloud-based computational resources to AWS customers. Some core AWS compute services are Amazon EC2, AWS Elastic Beanstalk, ELB, AWS Lambda, and Amazon ECS.
- Storage services provide cloud-based data storage to its customers. Some core AWS storage services are Amazon S3, Amazon EBS, AWS Snowball, AWS Storage Gateway, and Amazon EFS.
- Database services provide fully managed, cloud-based database resources to customers. Some core AWS database services are Amazon DynamoDB, Amazon RDS, Amazon Aurora, and Amazon Redshift.
- Network and content delivery services provide different ways for users and resources to access the AWS Cloud. Some core networking and content delivery services are AWS Direct Connect, Amazon Virtual Private Cloud, Amazon Virtual Private Network, Amazon CloudFront, AWS Global Accelerator, and Amazon Route 53.
- AWS management tools provide different ways to monitor and manage cloud resources on AWS. Some prominent tools are AWS CloudFormation, AWS CloudTrail, AWS Config, AWS CloudWatch, and AWS Trusted Advisor.

Chapter quiz answers

- 4.1.6: c. Elastic Load Balancing
  - *Answer*—Elastic Load Balancing automatically redistributes incoming web application traffic across multiple targets, such as Amazon EC2 instances, to help your web application increase availability.
- 4.2.6: b. Amazon Elastic Block Store
  - *Answer*—Amazon Elastic Block Store is a block-level storage volume to use with Amazon EC2 instances.
- 4.3.4: c. Amazon DynamoDB
  - *Answer*—Amazon Aurora and Amazon RDS are relational databases. Amazon DynamoDB is a NoSQL database.
- 4.4.2: b. IP Addresses
  - *Answer*—Amazon Route 53 translates human-readable names such google .com into IP addresses that connect computers and servers to each other.
- 4.5.6: d. AWS CloudFormation
  - *Answer*—AWS CloudFormation utilizes Infrastructure as Code to provision your IT infrastructure on AWS using code.

Security and compliance

This chapter covers
- Examining security and compliance concepts
- Learning about core security services

In chapter 4, we learned about the many different types of AWS Cloud services. They are compute services, storage services, database services, network and content delivery services, and management tools. Missing from the discussion was security services.

While many security concepts and services may take a back seat when compared with their more flashy counterparts like compute and storage services, security and compliance in the cloud are vital for architecting and maintaining effective and secure IT infrastructures.

Security and Compliance is also the second domain of the AWS Certified Cloud Practitioner exam. For those of you expecting to take the exam, chapter 7 covers the certification exam and the content you need to know in more detail. In the current chapter, we learn about vital security and compliance concepts and then move on to the core security services that you should know about when dipping your toes into the AWS Cloud.

5.1   *Security and compliance concepts*

When you think about security for your data and IT infrastructure, you may imagine a server room in the office, locked up with a card key that is carefully managed by the IT department, or perhaps an off-site data center that only select people can enter and exit. However, this image of securing data is quickly becoming replaced by cloud-based security, where the cloud computing service providers manage their own data centers on your behalf, including many aspects of data security, so that you can focus on other parts of IT infrastructure management.

Security and compliance in the cloud computing environment is one of the most important concepts for organizations and businesses to consider when deciding whether migrating their IT infrastructure to cloud computing platforms is a fit for them. As we learn throughout this chapter, keeping your cloud-based IT infrastructure secure and compliant is a shared responsibility between you (the customer) and the cloud computing platform.

When you decide to use AWS as your cloud computing platform, you can benefit from the dozens of compliance programs embedded into the platform to keep your data safe and meet your industry's and country's data security compliance requirements. AWS has a global network of data centers, architected with security in mind, so you can take advantage of all the safeguards in place to protect customers' privacy and ensure data security.

The security domain in the AWS Certified Cloud Practitioner exam, while smaller than other domains in number of questions, is important to understand because without security best practices and proper use of security services, you cannot have functional IT infrastructures. The security and compliance concepts we learn about in this section are as follows:

- The shared responsibility model
- The security pillar of AWS's Well-Architected Framework
- The principle of least privilege

5.1.1   *Shared responsibility model*

When a company uploads its IT infrastructure or data onto the AWS Cloud, who exactly is responsible for securing the data centers? The bits and bytes of data? The physical servers? The Amazon Elastic Compute Cloud (Amazon EC2) virtual server instances?

These are some of the important questions to grapple with as you evaluate whether running your IT operations on the cloud—in particular, on AWS Cloud—is the right decision for your organization. Thankfully, AWS helps you to deconstruct these questions by introducing the *shared responsibility model*.

As the name suggests, the shared responsibility model dictates that the responsibility for security of your IT resources hosted on the AWS Cloud is shared between the customer and AWS. However, AWS and the customer are responsible for different parts of cloud security. This delegation of responsibility is commonly broken down as follows:

- AWS is responsible for security of the cloud.
- The customer is responsible for security in the cloud.

AWS: SECURITY OF THE CLOUD

When it comes to sharing the responsibility of keeping your cloud computing resources secured, AWS is responsible for protecting the infrastructure that maintains and operates its services. These include the physical facilities housing all of the hardware, software, and networking that run AWS services.

AWS Cloud is responsible for the following:

- Hardware (physical security of data centers, physical servers, etc.)
- The AWS global infrastructure (Regions, Availability Zones, Edge Locations, etc.)

CUSTOMER: SECURITY IN THE CLOUD

The customer's responsibilities in keeping their cloud computing resources on AWS secure depend on which AWS Cloud services they are utilizing. Depending on how much configuration you must perform to set up and maintain your services, you will be responsible for different levels of security. Responsibilities may range from protecting the movement of data from beginning to end (encrypting data during data transfer) to making sure your virtual server's operating systems are patched and up to date.

The customer may be responsible for the following:

- Customer data
- Platform, applications, and identity and access management (IAM)
- Operating system, network, and firewall configuration
- Client-side data encryption and data integrity authentication
- Server-side encryption (file system and/or data)
- Networking traffic protection (encryption, integrity, identity)

You can think of security *of* the cloud as the security guard walking around the premises of a data center, keeping a lookout for potential threats, as well as making sure the physical hardware is well-protected and maintained.

Security *in* the cloud can be thought of as you, the customer—perhaps an employee accessing the data that's being protected inside the data center. The security guard can do their best to maintain the hardware's security, but if you don't do your part to keep your data secured—say, you leave passwords and usernames for virtual servers lying around—someone can hack into your systems and cause problems.

5.1.2 A Well-Architected Framework

We went over the AWS's Well-Architected Framework in chapter 2, where we learned about the six pillars that AWS defines for best practices in cloud computing. As you may recall, these six pillars are as follows:

- *Operational excellence*—Daily system operations, monitoring, and improvements
- *Security*—Protecting information and systems
- *Reliability*—Ability to prevent and quickly recover from operational failures
- *Performance efficiency*—Using computing resources efficiently
- *Cost optimization*—Avoiding unnecessary costs
- *Sustainability*—Continually improving sustainability impacts

Of these, we focus on the security pillar in this section. The security pillar, as you may imagine, describes how cloud computing technologies can protect data, systems, and assets.

SECURITY PILLAR

According to the security pillar of the AWS's Well-Architected Framework, security in the cloud is composed of five areas:

- IAM
- Detective controls
- Infrastructure protection
- Data protection
- Incident response

Establishing a strong identity foundation is vital for the proper management of user access to IT resources. To do this, you utilize the *principle of least privilege*, which we discuss in the next section.

People and other resources should only be given as much access as necessary to complete their jobs and roles and nothing more. Keeping data away from humans by eliminating the need for direct access or manual data processing is one of the best ways to keep data safe. By doing so, human error and loss or modification of sensitive data can be controlled or potentially eliminated entirely. You can enable detective controls by enabling traceability. This may come in the form of monitoring alerts, auditing actions, or monitoring changes to your environment in real time.

Your infrastructure should be protected on all layers instead of just on a single outer layer. If we're looking at an Amazon EC2 virtual server, this could mean that your cloud infrastructure is secured at the organizational, subnet, load balancer, virtual machine, and operating system layers.

Another way to add an extra layer of protection is to enable multifactor authentication (MFA) on your accounts. When you sign into your account, you're "authenticating" yourself, proving to the service that you are who you claim to be. Traditionally, this has been done through the use of usernames and passwords. Well, as you are probably aware from the numerous "Your account information has been compromised in the Deep Web" emails Gmail sends out about your saved passwords, a username and password combination is no longer enough to keep your accounts secured and to prove that the person trying to access your account is who they say they are.

Have a service that wants to send a verification code to your cellphone when you try to log in? Or are you asked to type in a code that's generated in your "authentication app" installed to your phone that updates itself every 30 or 60 seconds? Does your iPhone app require you to verify your identity via FaceID? If so, you are logging into an account that has MFA or two-step verification enabled! Requiring people to utilize MFA when logging into your services and accounts increases the security level of your environment by having the user enter a second factor to help verify their identity.

Data should be protected *at rest* (while it's being stored somewhere) and *in transit* (while it's moving from one place to another). The security mechanisms should be adjusted depending on the data's sensitivity level.

When a security event occurs, your team should be prepared to intervene, investigate, and deal with it promptly. This is referred to as *incident response*. Once the security event is resolved, the team should convene a postmortem (investigate what happened), update incident management processes, and learn from the event. The security pillar of the AWS's Well-Architected Framework is a vital part of creating and operating a stable and secure IT infrastructure.

5.1.3 *Principle of least privilege*

The *principle of least privilege*, also known as the *principle of minimal privilege* or the *principle of least authority*, is the concept that every user or program (called a *module*) should only be able to access information and resources necessary to complete their tasks or jobs successfully. As the name suggests, a module should only have the least amount of privilege necessary for its legitimate purpose.

If you are working in the marketing department of a company, it is unlikely that you require the same type of permissions someone in the IT department may require on a day-to-day basis to complete their work. You may have access to upload and edit files in the Marketing shared drive, but you may not be able to delete files other people in your department have uploaded. You most definitely should not be able to control who is granted access to the Marketing shared drive. However, someone working in IT who is responsible for provisioning or setting up the IT infrastructure and user access can change access permissions to different shared drive folders and files depending on the need.

Figure 5.1 illustrates this concept with Joe, the marketing manager of a consulting firm, and Jack, the firm's cafeteria's operations manager. Of these two, which person should be provided access to the company's marketing materials? The IT department needs to make sure that Joe, as the marketing manager, can access all necessary and relevant marketing resources. However, Jack, as the cafeteria operations manager, does not require access to these resources to complete his job. Providing Jack with access to these resources increases security risks to the company's proprietary information.

When I was working in IT years ago, one of my responsibilities was to efficiently provide and revoke access permissions to different resources so that users only had access to what they needed for their jobs. This can be especially important when users leave

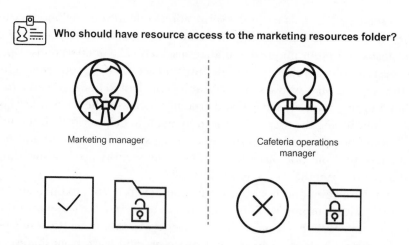

Figure 5.1   People and resources should only be given as much access as necessary to complete their jobs and nothing more.

the organization or company or switch to different teams. They should only have access to resources relevant to their work, which means that cutting off access when it's no longer needed should be swift and precise to prevent information misuse or loss.

In AWS, you may find yourself overwhelmed by the number of permissions you are required to consider and set for every service and feature you activate. While it's time-consuming and many times confusing, getting permissions correct is the key to securing your cloud IT infrastructure. AWS IAM is one of the ways you can effectively manage permissions to users and applications. We will go over this key service in more detail in the next section. For now, you can think of this service as a way to granularly set permissions for every module in your AWS Cloud infrastructure so that every user, application, and service only has the most appropriate amount of permissions necessary to complete their work.

You can also create *policies* to manage access to AWS resources. These policies can be attached to specific IAM identities (users, groups, or roles) or AWS resources (like services). A *policy* is an object that defines an identity's or resource's permissions. When an IAM principal (user or role) makes a request, AWS evaluates these policies to decide whether to allow the action.

There are six policy types:

- Identity-based policies
- Resource-based policies
- Permissions boundaries
- Organizations' service control policies
- Access control lists (ACLs)
- Session policies

While we won't go over them in any more detail in this book, you can check out this Knowledge Base article to learn more about each of these policy types and how you can utilize them to keep your AWS Cloud infrastructure secure: http://mng.bz/AVxe.

> **NOTE** You can learn more about the relationship between access management controlled by AWS IAM and policies here: http://mng.bz/ZpzN.

The principle of least privilege can get complicated as you become an AWS infrastructure engineer and begin controlling permissions and policies. For the purposes of this book and the AWS Certified Cloud Practitioner exam, you should know the most fundamental concept of the principle: *You should only grant as much access to resources and information as is necessary for the entity to successfully complete its work.*

5.1.4   Section quiz

In the shared responsibility model, AWS and the customer share responsibility for security. Which of the following is AWS responsible for?

- a   Server-side data encryption
- b   Physical servers
- c   Operating system patching
- d   Customer data
- e   Client-side data encryption

5.2   Security services

AWS security services assist you on your mission to secure your AWS Cloud's IT infrastructure. Each security-related service protects or monitors different parts of your infrastructure, allowing you to create a secure system by utilizing services that fit your organization's needs. In this section, we learn about these core security services:

- AWS IAM
- AWS Web Application Firewall (AWS WAF)
- AWS Shield
- Amazon Inspector
- AWS Trusted Advisor
- Amazon GuardDuty

5.2.1   AWS Identity and Access Management

AWS IAM provides you with fine-grained permissions to secure your AWS services and resources. You can utilize AWS IAM to specify who or what can access which services and resources. With IAM policies, you can protect your resources by utilizing the principle of least privilege. In a nutshell, AWS IAM allows you to define the following:

- Who (workforce users, workloads)
- Can access (permissions with IAM policies)
- What (resources)

Figure 5.2 illustrates AWS IAM. On the surface, IAM seems like a simple concept. However, as you begin building out your AWS Cloud IT infrastructure, you will likely realize that IAM is a big job. You can consider utilizing IAM Access Analyzer to help you set fine-grained permissions as your needs and security requirements evolve. It helps you navigate through the permissions management cycle of set, verify, and refine permissions to keep your IT infrastructure safe.

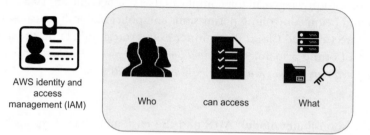

AWS identity and
access
management (IAM)   Who   can access   What

**Figure 5.2   AWS IAM
helps you define who
can access what.**

With IAM, you can manage AWS permission for *workforce users* (people, like employees, contractors, and partners) and *workloads* (a collection of resources and code that provide business value, like customer-facing applications). AWS recommends that you use AWS Single Sign-On to manage access to AWS accounts and permissions within those accounts for workforce users. For workload permissions, AWS recommends that you utilize IAM roles and policies to provide the least amount of required access. AWS IAM is free, and you can start using it as soon as you create an AWS Cloud account.

ROOT ACCOUNTS

When you sign up for your AWS account, you are provided a God-tier account. In other words, you have complete access to everything in that specific AWS account, including all the services and resources. This super-powered account is called the *AWS account root user.*

Given its sheer power, AWS does not recommend that you utilize the root account for everyday tasks (you wouldn't have the big boss come out to the frontlines in your RPG game to fight battles the foot soldiers can win, right?). AWS suggests that you use the root user (the original account that comes with the account) to create your first IAM user. The root user credentials should be locked away securely and only used to perform account and service management tasks as necessary.

> **Tasks that require use of the AWS account root user**
>
> Not everything can be done with an IAM user, no matter how many privileges you provide it. There are a few tasks that require the use of root user account:
>
> - Changing account settings (such as account name, email address, root user password, root access keys)
> - Restoring IAM user permissions
> - Activating IAM access to the Billing and Cost Management Console

- Viewing certain tax invoices
- Closing AWS account
- Changing or canceling an AWS support plan
- Registering as seller in Reserved Instance Marketplace
- Configuring MFA Delete for an Amazon Simple Storage Service bucket
- Editing or deleting an Amazon Simple Storage Service bucket policy that includes an invalid Virtual Private Cloud ID or Virtual Private Cloud endpoint ID
- Signing up for GovCloud (cloud platform for governments)

The tasks requiring root account access are explained in detail in this documentation: http://mng.bz/m21M.

Anyone who has access to the root user account has unrestricted access to all AWS resources in your account. Keep it tucked away safely!

5.2.2   AWS Web Application Firewall

AWS Web Application Firewall, or AWS WAF, is a firewall service for your web applications (don't you love it when the name is very to the point?). It protects web applications running on the AWS Cloud from common web exploits (such as SQL injections or cross-site scripting) that could potentially compromise the security or availability of your web applications. It also protects web applications from exploits that could force the applications to consume excessive resources (which means a lot of wasted money for you). As illustrated in figure 5.3, AWS WAF acts like a real-life firewall, creating a barrier between the "fire" (malicious web exploits) and your "rooms" (your resources hosted on AWS Cloud) so that your resources are protected.

Figure 5.3   AWS WAF is a firewall service for your web applications.

AWS WAF offers some nifty ways for you to protect your applications:

- Create custom web security rules to block common attack patterns.
- Deploy new rules in minutes so your web app is protected in real time.
- Control which traffic to allow or deny to your web apps with customized web security rules.
- Utilize the API to automate creation, deployment, and maintenance of web security rules.

AWS WAF improves web traffic visibility to and from your web applications, provides cost-effective web app protection, and increases security and protection against attacks. AWS WAF has no upfront costs; charges based on the number of web ACLs you create, the number of rules you add to these ACLs, and the number of web requests you receive.

NOTE   If you are interested in potentially utilizing AWS WAF and want to see what kind of financial impacts it may have on your organization, AWS provides a nifty pricing calculator to estimate your potential costs. It is available at https://aws.amazon.com/waf/pricing/.

5.2.3   *AWS Shield*

AWS Shield literally shields your applications running on the AWS Cloud from distributed denial-of-service (DDoS) attacks. A *DDoS attack* is a cybercrime in which an attacker (or attackers) floods a server with a huge amount of internet traffic to prevent legitimate users from accessing the website or online services. A server can only take so much traffic before it gets overwhelmed.

If you are in the United States, you might recall the failed Healthcare.gov website rollout for the Affordable Care Act (also known as Obamacare) in 2013. High demand for the website caused the website to go down within 2 hours of launch, preventing people looking to purchase health insurance from successfully accessing the federal exchange. While this service failure was caused by legitimate traffic, a DDoS attack can trigger the same phenomenon. Namely, a DDoS attack can overwhelm a server with internet traffic and make the services unavailable to the public (or legitimate traffic) or even cause the site to go offline (crash). As figure 5.4 shows, AWS Shield protects you by "shielding" your AWS resources, thus mitigating any potential damage caused by a DDoS attack.

With AWS Shield's always-on detection and automatic inline mitigations that help to minimize application downtime and latency, you can rely on real-time DDoS protection without needing to engage with AWS Support. There are two tiers to AWS Shield:

- AWS Shield Standard
- AWS Shield Advanced

Figure 5.4   AWS Shield protects your web applications running on the AWS Cloud from DDoS attacks.

All AWS customers can receive protection from AWS Shield Standard for free. AWS Shield Standard defends against common network and transport layer DDoS attacks on your website or application. When using AWS Shield Standard with Amazon Cloud-Front and Amazon Route 53, your web application is protected against all known infrastructure attacks (layers 3 and 4).

Subscribing to AWS Shield Advanced provides higher levels of protection against DDoS attacks that target your apps running on Amazon EC2, Elastic Load Balancing, Amazon CloudFront, AWS Global Accelerator, and Amazon Route 53. AWS Shield Advanced provides additional detection and mitigation against sophisticated DDoS attacks, near real-time visibility into DDoS attacks, and integration with AWS WAF, the web apps firewall service. You are also hooked up with 24/7 access to the AWS Shield Response Team. DDoS attacks often mean a spike in costs, as your server is bombarded with requests, so AWS Shield Advanced provides protection against DDoS-related charges.

5.2.4   *Amazon Inspector*

Amazon Inspector automatically inspects your AWS workloads for software vulnerabilities and potentially unintentional network exposures and brings them to your attention. It is an automated vulnerability management service that provides near real-time results. Amazon Inspector reduces the risk of introducing security issues during deployment and development. It proactively identifies potential issues that do not align with best practices and policies that you've defined. Amazon Inspector is available as a vulnerability management solution for Amazon EC2 and Amazon Elastic Container Registry.

Once an automated assessment of your applications is completed, Amazon Inspector generates detailed reports to help you check for unintended vulnerabilities that may cause security issues. Although you and your team can't be awake 24/7 to monitor for security vulnerabilities, Amazon Inspector can. That means you can get a good night's rest knowing your auditors and development team can rely on Amazon Inspector to adhere to security standards set by the company and the industry as a whole, day and night.

5.2.5   *AWS Trusted Advisor*

We went over AWS Trusted Advisor in section 4.5.5. We discussed how it is an IT auditor, checking off different ways to optimize your IT infrastructure to align with AWS's best practices. While AWS Trusted Advisor was featured in the "Management Tools" section of this book, it is also a security service because it performs checks to keep your IT infrastructure secure.

The categories of checks offered by AWS Trusted Advisor are as follows:

- Cost optimization
- Performance
- Security
- Fault tolerance
- Service quotas

Once the checks are complete, AWS Trusted Advisor provides recommendations to get your cloud IT infrastructure as close as possible to AWS best practices to keep it secure.

5.2.6   *Amazon GuardDuty*

Forget the night shift! Amazon has a security service that monitors for malicious activity and unauthorized behavior to protect your AWS Cloud instance 24/7 so you and your team can sleep. It's called Amazon GuardDuty. As the name suggests, it guards your (Cloud IT infrastructure) walls and is alert and on duty all day and all night. As mighty and trusty as it is, it only takes a few clicks to deploy, with no additional software or infrastructure to manage.

Figure 5.5 provides an image of how Amazon GuardDuty stands guard to protect your AWS Cloud resources from unauthorized behaviors and malicious activity 24/7. Once again, it's nice when you can decipher a service's role through its name.

Amazon GuardDuty utilizes machine learning, anomaly detection, and integrated threat intelligence to identify potential threats to your AWS Cloud IT infrastructure. It can even send actionable alerts via AWS CloudWatch Events so you take action immediately if a threat is detected. You can also integrate its findings into workflow systems and utilize AWS Lambda to automatically remediate or prevent certain threats. Have a

Figure 5.5 Amazon GuardDuty monitors your AWS Cloud instances for unauthorized behaviors and malicious activity.

good night's sleep knowing your AWS Cloud infrastructure is being guarded and monitored at all times!

5.2.7 Section quiz

To protect your applications from DDoS attacks, which AWS service would you utilize?

a AWS WAF

b Amazon GuardDuty

c AWS Shield

d AWS Trusted Advisor

e Amazon Inspector

Summary

- Security and compliance concepts are vital for creating and managing a secure IT infrastructure. Some of the core security and compliance concepts are the shared responsibility model, the security pillar of the AWS's Well-Architected Framework, and the principle of least privilege.
- The shared responsibility model states that you, the customer, and AWS Cloud share the responsibilities that come with keeping your cloud resources secured. AWS is responsible for security *of* the cloud, while the customer is responsible for security *in* the cloud.
- The security pillar of AWS's Well-Architected Framework states that security in the cloud is composed of IAM, detective controls, infrastructure protection, data protection, and incident response.

- The principle of least privilege states that people and resources should only be given as much access as necessary to complete their work and nothing more.
- Security is one of the four domains featured in the AWS Certified Cloud Practitioner exam, and while it is a smaller section than others, it is nonetheless a very important section to master.
- Some core security services you want to know about are AWS IAM, AWS Web Application Firewall (AWS WAF), AWS Shield, Amazon Inspector, AWS Trusted Advisor, and Amazon GuardDuty.

Chapter quiz answers

- 5.1.4: b. Physical servers
  - *Answer*—According to AWS's shared responsibility model for cloud security, AWS is responsible for the security *of* the cloud, and the customer is responsible for security *in* the cloud. Physical servers belong in security of the cloud, as they are managed in AWS's data centers.
- 5.2.7: c. AWS Shield
  - *Answer*—AWS Shield protects your applications running on AWS Cloud from DDoS attacks, which overwhelms your services with malicious requests in an attempt to make your website or online services unavailable.

Billing and pricing

This chapter covers

- Introducing the AWS Billing Dashboard
- Identifying the AWS pricing models
- Distinguishing consolidated billing, AWS cost calculators, and AWS Free Tier
- Examining the five AWS support plans

As you may recall, in chapter 5 we learned about foundational security and compliance concepts as well as many of the core AWS security services. We're getting to the end of the content section of this book with this chapter, where we introduce foundations of AWS's billing and pricing models, tools, and support plans.

6.1 AWS billing and pricing concepts

I won't lie—the idea of having to comprehend and then explain billing and pricing for AWS was an instant grimace-maker for me. I think many people experience similar reactions when they first encounter the seemingly endless ways AWS can charge for each service and how monthly costs are calculated. Social media is filled with posts about nasty billing surprises some organization or person had when checking their monthly AWS bill.

Although understanding and managing billing and cost analyses with cloud computing is not an easy feat, AWS offers many resources and tools to help you decipher your monthly cloud bills. It's still not simple, but these tools and resources may make the process of understanding and anticipating your monthly AWS bills a little easier. In this section, we first learn about core billing and pricing concepts such as

- Types of AWS pricing models
- AWS Free Tier

We also evaluate several tools and resources that AWS provides to help you navigate your AWS bills:

- AWS Billing Dashboard (inside the AWS Billing Console)
- Consolidated billing
- AWS cost calculators

To make this a little more fun (because it can be rather dry), let's imagine that you are an IT director at a medium-sized startup. You are evaluating whether to migrate your IT infrastructure to the AWS Cloud. Consider how you might use each tool to get some valuable information that will allow you and your organization to make effective business decisions. Let's get started!

6.1.1 *Types of AWS pricing models*

One of the biggest benefits to utilizing AWS and cloud computing in general is that cloud computing offers a pay-as-you-go pricing model as opposed to the pay-full-price-before-you-use model we're used to with legacy on-premises (on-site) IT infrastructure purchases. As we discussed earlier, you can think of the AWS payment system like your monthly utility bills for water and electricity.

Rather than paying $2500 up front for that MacBook Pro, you can spin up a virtual machine on AWS and pay monthly usage fees for the resources you consumed, for as long as you use them. When you no longer need the service, you can shut it down, and you are no longer charged. While that seems simple enough, there is actually a bit more granularity in how AWS pricing works, which you need to know before spinning up different AWS services. Let's take a look.

FUNDAMENTALS OF AWS PRICING

Depending on the services you are utilizing, they may be billed differently. Some examples are per GB of storage with Amazon Simple Cloud Storage (Amazon S3) and per hour of use with Amazon Elastic Compute Cloud (Amazon EC2). You can check out the different ways services are priced by scrolling to Services Pricing on the AWS Pricing page (https://aws.amazon.com/pricing/) and clicking the desired service category. As illustrated in figure 6.1, the fundamental drivers of cost with AWS (how you are charged for utilizing AWS) are as follows:

- Compute
- Storage
- Outbound data transfer (inbound data transfer is generally free)

Figure 6.1 The three fundamental ways you can be charged for utilizing AWS Cloud are compute, storage, and outbound data transfer.

> **NOTE** Another great resource is an AWS white paper titled "How AWS Pricing Works: AWS Pricing Overview," which can be viewed at http://mng.bz/RvER.

AWS'S PRICING MODELS

AWS also has several pricing models that incentivize planning in advance and consuming more resources. Including the pay-as-you-go model we've already discussed, AWS's pricing models are as follows:

- *Pay as you go (on-demand pricing)*—This is the most flexible pricing plan: you only pay for what you use without overcommitting budgets, and it is responsive to granular changes in requirements.
- *Save when you commit (reserved instances)*—Utilize savings plans by committing to using a specific amount of an AWS service or category of services for a one- or three-year period.
- *Take advantage of unused AWS capacity (spot instances)*—Receive huge discounts compared to on-demand pricing when you use unutilized AWS capacity (Amazon EC2 spot instances are up to 90% off on-demand pricing!).
- *Pay less by using more*—Receive volume discounts as your usage increases with tiered pricing for certain services (generally requires *a lot* of resource use).

By mixing and matching these different pricing models with your organization's specific needs, you can get the most bang for your buck while retaining flexibility and responsiveness in critical areas.

As a quick example, you may choose to spin up your virtual servers on Amazon EC2 with pay-as-you-go pricing for new projects. You are still scoping out your needs and want to retain flexibility, so you go with on-demand pricing. However, you decide to commit to a certain amount of Amazon S3 storage for 1- and 3-year periods for storing backups. You have a fairly good grasp of your backup needs, so you feel confident about committing to a savings plan for some storage to save a bit of money.

Figure 6.2 illustrates how the pay-less-by-using-more pricing model may work with Amazon S3, AWS Cloud's major storage service:

- With Amazon S3 Standard, when you utilize up to 50 TB of storage, your storage cost is $0.023 per GB/month (as of Summer 2022).
- Your next 450 TB of storage is priced at $0.022 per GB/month.
- For storage of data over 500 TB, you are charged $0.021 per GB/month.

NOTE   If you are interested in learning more about Amazon S3 pricing, you can head over to https://aws.amazon.com/s3/pricing/.

While, at a glance, $0.023 per GB versus $0.022 or $0.021 per GB doesn't seem like a big difference, remember that 1 TB of data is the same as 1024 GB of data, and we're talking about potentially hundreds of terabytes of data being stored in S3!

Amazon S3 Standard pricing by storage size

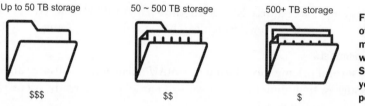

Up to 50 TB storage   50 ~ 500 TB storage   500+ TB storage

$$$ $$ $

Figure 6.2   An example of the pay-less-by-using-more pricing model at work with Amazon S3 Standard, where the more you store, the less you pay per gigabyte of storage

6.1.2   *AWS Free Tier*

The AWS Free Tier is a robust and generous program that is automatically activated on each new AWS account for 12 months (in cases of some services, forever). It allows you to try out more than 100 AWS products for free up to a specific maximum usage amount each month. If you go over the usage limits, such as going over the 5 GB storage limit for Amazon S3's Free Tier in the first 12 months, you are charged the normal rate for the overage. One thing to keep in mind is that not all AWS services are covered under the AWS Free Tier, so to avoid unexpected bills, you should check your selected services before spinning them up.

NOTE   You can find out what services are covered by the AWS Free Tier and their limits at https://aws.amazon.com/free/.

TYPES OF AWS FREE TIER OFFERINGS

The AWS Free Tier has three different types of offerings:

- *Trials*—Short-term trials where you pay standard rates after the trial periods end (for example, a 30-day free trial for 10 GB of SPICE capacity for Amazon QuickSight)

- *12 months free*—Free limited use for 12 months after your account sign-up date (for example, 5 GB of standard storage, 20,000 Get requests, and 2,000 Put requests for 12 months for Amazon S3)
- *Always free*—Offers available with no expiration to all AWS customers (for example, 1 million free requests and 3.2 million seconds of compute time per month for AWS Lambda)

Even if a service is covered by the AWS Free Tier, it could be under any of the three vastly different offering types, so it is very important to confirm with the official AWS Free Tier website before using any of the AWS products you're interested in.

The AWS Free Tier is great for both beginners and experienced cloud engineers to experiment with different AWS services, learn how they work and how they are billed, and test out different ways of architecting in the cloud. For those of you looking to take the AWS Certified Cloud Practitioner exam, or perhaps one of the more specialized exams, or who want to pursue a career in cloud computing, it's a vital tool to begin dabbling with AWS. As they say, there is no better teacher than experience! You can read about AWS and its services, but you can't beat a few hours poking around in the AWS console and playing with different services.

While you need to watch out for some constraints to avoid unexpected charges at the end of the month, the AWS Free Tier is a great way to start engaging with the AWS Cloud and try out many of the services and features we've been learning about throughout this book. Just make sure you're also utilizing the tools we go over in the rest of the chapter to monitor your usage!

6.1.3   AWS Billing Dashboard

The AWS Billing Dashboard provides a general view of your AWS spending and usage. The AWS Billing Dashboard is the default main page of the AWS Billing Console. The navigation bar to the left of the dashboard allows you to navigate through the other AWS Billing Console tools, such as billing information, cost management tools, and user preferences.

If you are utilizing the AWS Free Tier, keeping tabs on your AWS resource usage through the AWS Billing Console may be especially helpful, as knowing the limits to free usage and monitoring your resources can prevent unwanted bills. (It's also great practice for the "real world" once you are more committed to utilizing AWS and need to keep track of all of your organization's usages.)

As figure 6.3 illustrates, the AWS Billing Dashboard brings together different pieces of information that may be relevant to your organization's (billing) interests. You can, for example, view your AWS summary, with the current month's total forecast, number of active services, current month-to-date balance, active AWS accounts, and trends comparing your current month's usage with the previous month's usage.

Other dashboard items that come as a default are the highest cost panel, which shows you the highest service spending for the current month; cost trends by the top

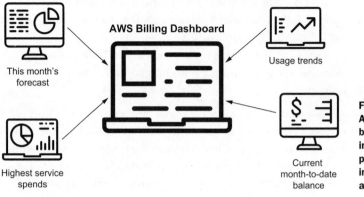

Figure 6.3   The AWS Billing Dashboard brings together different informational panels to provide you with valuable insights on your AWS bill and resource usage.

five services over a three-month period; and account cost trends with data over a three-month period.

While these panels are the defaults, the AWS Billing Dashboard is customizable so you can see the information that's uniquely important to you when you log in. This Knowledge Base documentation proves an overview of the AWS Billing Dashboard and the information you can glean from a quick glance: http://mng.bz/19oQ.

> **NOTE**   Already have an AWS account and want to check out the AWS Billing Dashboard? You can find it here after logging in: https://console.aws.amazon.com/billing/.

6.1.4   *Consolidated billing*

Do you have multiple AWS accounts for your company or organization and wish you could view and pay all of your monthly bills from one central location instead of logging into each account? Consolidated billing is your new best friend!

Consolidated billing allows *consolidated* payments (wink wink) from multiple AWS accounts within an organization, called *linked accounts*, by a single designated billing/accounting account, called the *management account*. This account can only be used for accounting and billing purposes, so don't try to spin up any virtual servers using a management account.

Here are a few quick notes about consolidated billing, linked accounts, and management accounts:

- Management accounts cannot access data within linked accounts.
- Management accounts are billed for all linked account charges, but each linked account is an independent account.
- Management accounts receive a combined view of monthly charges for all linked accounts, but this is strictly an accounting/billing feature.
- Management accounts cannot control linked accounts or provision AWS resources to them.

- After you "create" your organization in the AWS Organization Console, you can create accounts, which automatically become members of your organization, or you can you can invite existing accounts to join your organization.
- You may be able to share volume pricing discounts by combining usage across all accounts (potentially saving you a lot of money!).

As you'd expect, you can track charges across multiple AWS accounts and understand the combined cost and usage data. Instead of paying multiple bills, you get just one bill for all of your accounts. And it's free to use!

Aside from these perks, there is another pretty impactful benefit to using consolidated billing: combined usage! By combining resource usage across all AWS linked accounts within your organization and treating them all as one account, you may be able to take advantage of volume pricing discounts, reserved instance discounts, and savings plans. As a result, your organization may incur lower charges overall compared to paying for each individual AWS account separately.

Are you interested in how volume discounts work and how they might affect your organization? Check out this AWS Knowledge Base article on volume discounts: http://mng.bz/Pon8.

> **NOTE** Have multiple AWS accounts and want to use consolidated billing to make your accounting life easier and take advantage of potential volume discounts? You can check out this Knowledge Base documentation to set it up: http://mng.bz/JV2z.

6.1.5 *AWS cost calculators*

AWS offers a variety of cost/pricing calculators and other ways to help you save money or analyze your resource usage and bills. While this is not an exhaustive list of these tools, it should help you to start analyzing costs associated with establishing and operating your IT infrastructure on the AWS Cloud.

The tools we discuss in this section are as follows:

- AWS Pricing Calculator
- AWS Simple Monthly Calculator
- Migration Evaluator
- AWS Budgets
- AWS Cost Explorer
- AWS Cost and Usage Report (CUR)
- Amazon QuickSight

And they're all free, except Amazon QuickSight (sorry!). But all the other tools are free! Let's take a look.

AWS PRICING CALCULATOR

The AWS Pricing Calculator, which has more or less replaced the AWS Total Cost of Ownership Calculator, has a nifty short URL: https://calculator.aws/. When you enter the AWS services you want to utilize in your AWS infrastructure, along with estimates of your resource usage, the AWS Pricing Calculator creates a cost estimate for you. The cost estimate is broken down per service and per service group to give you a better overview of where the money goes. It also provides you with the total estimated cost for your infrastructure as a whole.

Using the AWS Pricing Calculator is like creating a mock monthly budget for your life. Plug in all your needs and wants (things like rent, gym membership, utilities, car insurance, and gasoline) and how much you plan on using them. For example, how much do you plan on grocery shopping versus eating out? Are you home all day and use a lot of electricity, or are you at work most of the time and can save a bit on heating/cooling? Given this information, a cost calculator can estimate your monthly personal budget. Similarly, the AWS Pricing Calculator will spit out an estimated monthly budget for utilizing the AWS Cloud. This calculator is a great tool when you are deciding whether moving your organization's IT infrastructure to the AWS Cloud could potentially save you money or if you're considering ramping up or down your resource usage and want to see the potential cost implications.

Figure 6.4 shows how the AWS Pricing Calculator takes the AWS services you want to utilize, along with the details of how you want to configure and use the services, and provides you with the estimated costs associated with running these workloads on the AWS Cloud.

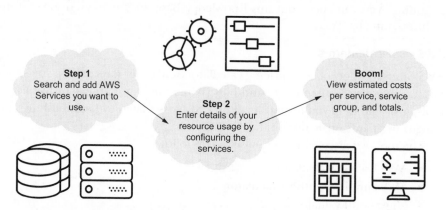

Figure 6.4   The AWS Pricing Calculator takes your input and calculates estimated costs for running your workloads on AWS.

The AWS Pricing Calculator shows the transparent pricing and math that go into estimating the cost of your service configurations. You can also share this information with your team using a unique link or exported .csv or .pdf files.

AWS SIMPLE MONTHLY CALCULATOR

The AWS Pricing Calculator will also soon be replacing the AWS Simple Monthly Calculator, which can still be accessed here (as of Summer 2022): https://calculator.s3.amazonaws.com/index.html. The Simple Monthly Calculator is an online tool that allows you to estimate the monthly cost of various AWS services based on your unique expected use-case scenarios. Like with the AWS Pricing Calculator, you can use the AWS Simple Monthly Calculator to create mock monthly budgets for your IT infrastructure just as you would for your own life.

In the navigation bar to the left of the AWS Simple Monthly Calculator website dashboard, you can select the AWS service you are interested in. After adding your expected usages in your preferred Region, you receive an estimated monthly bill that you can then export, save, or share.

MIGRATION EVALUATOR

The Migration Evaluator (previously known as TSO Logic) creates data-driven business cases for planning and migrating your IT infrastructure to the AWS Cloud. You can utilize its tools to monitor your current resource usages on your infrastructure. In addition, a team of program managers and solutions architects at AWS can evaluate your migration objectives and recommend methodologies that best suit your migration needs. The results are then provided as a business case you can take to your stakeholders to get that migration project approved!

While you may only consider accessing this tool if you are on a migration team evaluating whether moving your IT infrastructure to the AWS Cloud is a plausible business decision, it's still good to know about in case it comes up in a conversation. You can learn more about how the Migration Evaluator (and the white-gloved team!) may help you to develop a stellar business case for your organization's IT migration into the AWS Cloud here: https://aws.amazon.com/migration-evaluator/.

AWS BUDGETS

As with household budgets, an AWS infrastructure budget is most effective when you create it before you spend. With AWS Budgets, you can set custom budgets to track your AWS resource usage and costs associated with your infrastructure.

For example, I use Mint, a budgeting app for personal finances. When my food bills start getting a little too close to my ideal budget amount, Mint shoots me an email alerting me that I may need to ease up on my takeout meals for the remainder of the month. Similarly, AWS Budgets can send you an alert when actual or forecasted usage nears or exceeds your budget threshold.

You can even configure certain actions to execute automatically (or with your approval) when cost or usage exceeds or is forecasted to exceed your threshold so that you don't end up with a surprise bill at the end of the month. You can check out the benefits of the AWS Budgets tool here: http://mng.bz/wyoB.

AWS COST EXPLORER

If AWS Budgets is helpful to estimate costs *before* you spend, the AWS Cost Explorer is helpful for visualizing and analyzing your AWS Cloud costs *after* you spend. It's like pulling out all of your credit card bills and bank statements and analyzing what you actually spent so you determine whether the monthly budget you set for yourself was accurate or you need to adjust your expectations and your budget to better align with your day-to-day expenses.

Setting a budget is great, but it's useless if you don't follow it or if it's completely inaccurate! (I always think I'll spend way less on food than I end up spending, so I finally decided to accept that fact and change my budget to cut down on other things that aren't as important to me to make the numbers add up.)

Once you receive your AWS Cloud bill for the previous month, you can head over to the AWS Cost Explorer to get custom analysis reports of your AWS cost and usage data. Once you have enough data points, you can also analyze AWS Cloud costs and usages over time. With enough data under your belt, the tool can also forecast future costs and usage so your organization can plan ahead.

The AWS Cost Explorer provides you with a bird's-eye-view of the analysis, such as the total cost across all accounts, or it can take a deep dive into different aspects of AWS Cloud resource usage to identify data trends and cost drivers or detect anomalies that may indicate something amiss. If you want to learn more about how the AWS Cost Explorer works and what information and insight it can provide you and your organization, hop over to this link: http://mng.bz/qoYN.

AWS COST AND USAGE REPORT

As the name suggests, AWS Cost and Usage Report (CUR) provides a comprehensive set of AWS cost and usage data so organizations can understand cost drivers and identify ways to optimize their monthly AWS usage bills. The CUR includes metadata (data about data) on the following:

- AWS services
- Pricing
- Credits
- Fees
- Taxes
- Discounts
- Cost categories
- Reserved instances
- Savings plans

You can integrate the information generated by CUR with Amazon Athena, Amazon Redshift, or Amazon QuickSight for querying cost and usage information for further analysis.

The generated reports are free, but they are stored in Amazon S3 buckets, which may cost a few pennies each month depending on your overall usage. If you want to take a look at the AWS CUR, you can do so through this link: http://mng.bz/7ZyV.

AMAZON QUICKSIGHT

If the Amazon Billing Dashboard helps you to visualize your AWS usages, costs, and trends, Amazon QuickSight does so for your organization's data. You can connect all of your data residing in AWS, third-party cloud platforms, or your on-premises infrastructure to create complex data models and visualizations. Amazon QuickSight provides customizable dashboards that are completely use-case specific for you, your developers, your end users, or anyone else you want to create data-based dashboards for.

In addition to being a tool you can use to visualize your AWS billing or cost-related information to keep track of your monthly bills, Amazon QuickSight has many other functions. For example, through machine learning, it can find trends and provide valuable insights into all sorts of data (including your AWS resource usage and bills). It's not free, but you can get started with a free trial. For sample dashboards and more information about Amazon QuickSight, check out the introduction page at https:// aws.amazon.com/quicksight/.

6.1.6   Section quiz

Which one of the following is *not* a benefit of consolidated billing with AWS?

   a   You can receive one bill for all linked accounts within an organization.
   b   You can receive volume discounts for the organization as a whole.
   c   You can set up a super-admin management account to manage all linked accounts and their resources.
   d   The management account can pay for combined monthly charges for all linked accounts.

6.2   AWS support plans

With any robust and comprehensive service come support plans to keep the infrastructure running smoothly and to troubleshoot when issues arise. AWS has tiered support plans at vastly varying price points to fit your organization's level of need and budget.

Phrases like "a 30-day money back guarantee" and "24/7 technical support" help us feel more confident about trying out something new or making a leap-of-faith purchase. When you need the help, having access to great support services that solve your issues quickly and effectively can make a huge difference in how you perceive the company as well as your satisfaction with your purchase.

For AWS, technical support (and, after a point, proactive architectural support) comes at price points that vary widely depending on your organization's needs, use case, and budget. AWS offers five types of support plans that are unique in scope and cost (from $0/month to "starting from" $15,000/month). As outlined here and shown in table 6.1, these support plan types are as follows:

   - The Basic Support Plan
   - The Developer Support Plan
   - The Business Support Plan
   - The Enterprise On-Ramp Support Plan
   - The Enterprise Support Plan

Yeah, these pricing schemes are quite overwhelming, especially when you are encountering them for the first time. Let's go over each support plan, how much it costs, what

Table 6.1   Basic overview of AWS support plans

The Basic Support Plan	The Developer Support Plan	The Business Support Plan
For testing out/experimenting with AWS (great for the AWS Free Tier) ■ Free	For testing out/experimenting with AWS Greater of: ■ $29 *or* ■ 3% of your monthly AWS charges	Minimum recommendation for those with production workloads in AWS Greater of: ■ $100 *or* ■ 10% of your monthly AWS charges for first $0~10,000 ■ 7% of monthly AWS charges from $10,000~$80,000 ■ 5% of monthly AWS charges from $80,000~$250,000 ■ 3% of monthly AWS charges over $250,000

The Enterprise On-Ramp Support Plan	The Enterprise Support Plan
For those with production and/or business critical workloads in AWS Greater of: ■ $5,500 *or* ■ 10% of your monthly AWS charges	For those with business and/or mission critical workloads in AWS Greater of: ■ $15,000 *or* ■ 10% of your monthly AWS charges for first $0~$150,000 ■ 7% of monthly AWS charges from $150,000~$500,000 ■ 5% of monthly AWS charges from $500,000~$1 million ■ 3% of monthly AWS charges over $1 million

it does for you as the customer, and how to compare and contrast the plans to select one that fits your organization's needs. Onwards!

6.2.1   *The Basic Support Plan*

The Basic Support Plan only offers account and billing questions support and service quota increase requests. When you sign up for an AWS account, you are automatically set up with free basic features of this support plan with 24/7 access. The Basic Support Plan features are as follows:

- 1:1 response for account and billing inquiries
- Access to support forums, like AWS re:Post (https://www.repost.aws/)
- Service health checks (remember the AWS Trusted Advisor from the last chapter?)
- Access to documentation, technical papers, and best-practice guides
- Access to AWS Health Dashboard (http://mng.bz/m2Oy)

WHO MIGHT USE THIS SUPPORT PLAN?

A target demographic for the Basic Support Plan might be a developer wanting to test out different AWS services and how they could benefit the developer's career or side hustle. Another target demographic may be you, as a reader of this book, looking to get hands-on experience with the AWS user interface and different core services as you learn about them. Another potential customer for this plan might be someone considering moving their organization's IT infrastructure to the cloud and is in the process of evaluating different platforms, including AWS.

In general, this support plan is great for people who are testing out AWS but have no production workloads hosted on AWS Cloud. This support plan combines very nicely with the AWS Free Tier we learned about in section 6.1.2.

6.2.2   *The Developer Support Plan*

You can't expect very much in terms of technical support from the Basic Support Plan beyond posting on forums and hoping for a nuanced response. When you're ready to commit a little more to building and architecting in the AWS Cloud but are not ready for the sticker shock of a fancy support plan price, you can check out the Developer Support Plan.

In addition to the resources accessible via the Basic Support Plan, you get the following features with the Developer Support Plan:

- Best-practices guidance
- Access to client-side diagnostic tools
- Access to building-block architecture support that provides guidance on how to utilize the different AWS products, features, and services together effectively
- Ability to have an unlimited number of open support cases via one primary contact (your AWS account's *root user*)
- Business-hours email access to Cloud Support Associates
- Support response times of <24 hours for general guidance and <12 hours for system impaired
- Prioritized responses on AWS re:Post
- Access to Support Automation Workflows with prefixes *AWSSupport* (learn more here: http://mng.bz/5mQZ)

PRICING MODEL FOR THE DEVELOPER SUPPORT PLAN

The pricing model for the Developer Support Plan is a monthly fee that is the greater of

- $29 *or*
- 3% of your monthly AWS charges

These charges are in addition to your monthly AWS resource use charges.

WHO MIGHT USE THIS SUPPORT PLAN?

This support plan is great for developers and IT departments who are building their IT infrastructure on the AWS Cloud but are still in the experimental phase. While the plan offers more customized support with the ability to open tickets with 12- or 24-hour support response times and email access to Cloud Support Associates, it's not ideal for those organizations or people with production workloads. If something goes wrong, this plan's level of support may not be enough—or quick enough—to resolve problems in a timely manner, especially if an organization has angry customers waiting for answers. While it's not free like the Basic Support Plan, this is a great choice for developers looking for a bit more support from AWS but are not willing to commit to a hefty support bill month to month.

6.2.3 *The Business Support Plan*

When you've moved on from testing and experimenting on AWS to running production workloads (think: stuff your customers can see or use, such as your company's website or web applications), it may be time to consider upgrading your support plan to the Business Support Plan. In addition to the resources and services offered by the Basic Support Plan and the Developer Support Plan, the Business Support Plan provides the following features:

- Access to use-case guidance that helps you map out what AWS products features and services you should utilize to support your specific needs
- Ability to utilize a full set of checks with the AWS Trusted Advisor's Best Practice Checks (instead of the basic checks offered for the Basic Support Plan and the Developer Support Plan)
- Access to the AWS Support API to interact with an AWS Trusted Advisor and the Support Center, allowing you to automate support case management with an AWS Trusted Advisor via the API
- Interoperability and configuration troubleshooting for popular third-party software components on AWS and Amazon EC2 operating systems
- Ability for an unlimited number of AWS Identity and Access Management users to open an unlimited number of technical support cases (no longer just the root user as in the Developer Support Plan)
- 24/7 phone, email, and chat access to AWS Cloud Support Engineers
- Support response times: <24 hours for general guidance, <12 hours for system impaired, <4 hours for production system impaired, and <1 hour for production system down
- Access to Support Automation Workflows with prefixes *AWSSupport* and *AWSPremiumSupport*
- Infrastructure Event Management, for an additional fee (for more information, see http://mng.bz/69XZ)

PRICING MODEL FOR THE BUSINESS SUPPORT PLAN

The pricing model for the Business Support Plan is a monthly fee that is the greater of

- $100 *or*
- 10% of your monthly AWS charges for first $0 to $10,000
- 7% of monthly AWS charges from $10,000 to $80,000
- 5% of monthly AWS charges from $80,000 to $250,000
- 3% of monthly AWS usage over $250,000

As you can see, if your AWS account's workload is not very large (monthly usage charges of <$10,000), you may get away with $100 to $1,000 in monthly support plan costs when you sign on with the Business Support Plan. But as your monthly AWS charges increase, so does your support plan bill. Keep in mind that this support plan fee is in addition to your monthly usage fee. Thankfully, AWS utilizes the pay-less-by-using-more pricing model concept we learned about earlier (see section 6.1.1), so the percentage you pay goes down as you utilize more resources (for example, 5% of monthly AWS charges from $80,000–$250,000 vs just 3% for usage over $250,000).

WHO MIGHT USE THIS SUPPORT PLAN?

As the name of this support plan suggests, the target audience for the Business Support Plan is organizations with business needs, running production workloads on AWS, that require more customized support with faster response times when things go awry. While the offerings are not as robust as the next few support plans, this plan does provide use-case guidance to help you build your IT infrastructure in AWS to fit your specific business needs.

The pricing model is slightly more complicated than the previously discussed plans. Once you begin paying thousands of dollars every month for the Business Support Plan because of the growing cost of your monthly AWS usages, it may be time to consider upgrading to the Enterprise On-Ramp Support Plan to receive more benefits for potentially similar support plan prices.

6.2.4   *The Enterprise On-Ramp Support Plan*

Released for general availability in Fall 2021, the Enterprise On-Ramp Support Plan is a new support tier between the Business Support Plan and the Enterprise Support Plan. This support plan may be beneficial for organizations who have more support needs than what the Business Support Plan can provide but perhaps are not ready to pay (at least) $15,000 per month for the Enterprise Support Plan. The Enterprise On-Ramp Support Plan provides support for organizations with business-critical workloads hosted on the AWS Cloud.

In addition to the features that come with the Basic Support Plan, the Developer Support Plan, and the Business Support Plan, customers who enroll in the Enterprise On-Ramp Support Plan benefit from following features:

- Access to consultative application architecture guidance on how AWS services and resources fit together to meet your specific use case
- Access to short-term engagement with AWS Support to receive architectural and scaling guidance for Infrastructure Event Management once a year (available for a fee with the Business Support Plan)
- Access to a pool of Technical Account Managers (TAMs) to support your specific use cases and applications, provide proactive guidance, and coordinate support through programs and AWS experts
- White-gloved case routing via the Concierge Support Team

- Access to management business reviews
- Support response times: <24 hours for general guidance, <12 hours for system impaired, <4 hours for production system impaired, <1 hour for production system down, and <30 minutes for business-critical system down

PRICING MODEL FOR THE ENTERPRISE ON-RAMP SUPPORT PLAN

The pricing model for the Enterprise On-Ramp Support Plan is a monthly fee that is the greater of

- $5,500 *or*
- 10% of your monthly AWS charges

This pricing model is much simpler than the Business Support Plan or Enterprise Support Plan, and the least expensive option of $5,500 per month is much cheaper than the Enterprise Support Plan, which begins at $15,000 per month.

However, since the costs are not tiered and are instead charged at a flat rate of 10% of your monthly AWS charges, once your organization's monthly spend on the AWS Cloud begins growing, you will want to reevaluate whether this support plan is the most cost-effective option of the two enterprise-level plans. If you are constantly paying more than $15,000 a month for your support plan, it might be time to upgrade to the Enterprise Support Plan and receive the perks that come with this Ferrari-grade plan!

WHO MIGHT USE THIS SUPPORT PLAN?

With the Enterprise On-Ramp Support Plan, we are entering the realm of white-gloved service for premium pricings. Until recently, there was a huge jump from the Business Support Plan to the Enterprise Support Plan, both in the level of support and resources offered and the associated costs. In Fall 2021, AWS announced the Enterprise On-Ramp Support Plan as a stepping stone between the two plans. It offers attractive services like access to TAMs and the Concierge Support Team, as well as architectural guidance, at a much more affordable rate than that of the Enterprise Support Plan.

Given the high needs and the high costs associated with entering into an agreement with AWS to provide you with this support plan, your organization is likely spending *a lot* of money running production-level and business-critical IT infrastructure on the AWS Cloud. When problems arise, you need efficient, white-gloved support and very fast responses for production and business-critical system-down issues.

6.2.5 *The Enterprise Support Plan*

The Enterprise Support Plan is meant for organizations with business- and/or mission-critical workloads hosted on the AWS Cloud, and the price tag reflects the seriousness of this engagement. The features you receive with the Enterprise Support Plan are very similar to what you receive with the Enterprise On-Ramp Support Plan, but for the extra costs associated with this plan, you also receive the following benefits: ·

- Infrastructure Event Management (not limited to one a year as in the Enterprise On-Ramp Support Plan)
- Access to proactive workshops, reviews, and deep dives for your organization (learn more about AWS's proactive support services here: http://mng.bz/o522)
- Assigned to a designated TAM to proactively monitor and assist with optimization for your AWS Cloud environment, as well as coordinate access to AWS experts and relevant programs for your organization
- Access to online self-paced labs for employee training
- Support response times: <24 hours for general guidance, <12 hours for system impaired, <4 hours for production system impaired, <1 hour for production system down, and <15 minutes for business- and/or mission-critical system down

PRICING MODEL FOR ENTERPRISE SUPPORT PLAN

The pricing model for the Enterprise Support Plan is a monthly fee that is the greater of

- $15,000 (I know right?) *or*
- 10% of your monthly AWS charges for first $0 to $150,000
- 7% of monthly AWS charges from $150,000 to $500,000
- 5% of monthly AWS charges from $500,000 to $1 million
- 3% of monthly AWS charges over $1 million

These are monthly charges (phew)! The numbers just go up and up! As you might imagine, this support plan is for super-heavy users and are not to be taken lightly. As mentioned earlier, your support plan bill is in addition to your monthly AWS usage bill.

EXAMPLE OF AN ENTERPRISE SUPPORT PLAN CHARGE CALCULATION

The numbers are getting rather large, so let's see an example calculation for monthly AWS charges of $1.1 million:

- 10% of your monthly AWS charges for first $0 to $150,000: $150,000 × 10% = $15,000
- 7% of monthly AWS charges from $150,000 to $500,000: $350,000 × 7% = $24,500
- 5% of monthly AWS charges from $500,000 to $1 million: $500,000 × 5% = $25,000
- 3% of monthly AWS charges over $1 million: $100,000 × 3% = $3,000
- Total: $15,000 + $24,500 + $25,000 + $3,000 = $67,500

Since the $67,500 is higher than the minimum support bill of $15,000, you will pay $67,500 for the Enterprise Support Plan in addition to the $1.1 million for AWS usage. Wow! This is definitely not a support plan to be signed onto lightly. I wish this was my monthly royalty statement (I kid! I kid! No, wait, I'm serious.).

WHO MIGHT USE THIS SUPPORT PLAN?

Entities subscribing to the Enterprise Support Plan are likely huge organizations with extremely large operational costs for their IT infrastructure (possibly in the millions per month). They need a lot of proactive and fire-fighting support from AWS to both optimize their IT infrastructure and mitigate any issues that arise.

These organizations are running business- and/or mission-critical infrastructure on AWS and need highly customized and extremely efficient support with very short response times. Like with the Enterprise On-Ramp Support Plan, they have access to a TAM, but when you pay this much, you get assigned a designated TAM who proactively monitors your AWS Cloud environment to help you optimize. Now that's white-gloved service!

As reiterated many times, the support plan costs are in addition to AWS usage costs. In other words, the Enterprise Support Plan is going to cost you quite a bit on top of (likely) millions of dollars a month in cloud computing expenses, so it's not for the faint of heart. Or, perhaps, you are anxious and have a huge operational budget; if so, this is definitely the plan to sign up for, to make sure you're taken care of when something unexpected occurs!

6.2.6   *Evaluating support plan options*

AWS offers a handy table to compare and contrast the premium support plan options on its website (https://aws.amazon.com/premiumsupport/plans/). The Basic Support Plan isn't included in this list, as it's technically not a "premium support plan." However, for your own knowledge, and for the purpose of studying for the AWS Certified Cloud Practitioner exam, the table on that web page is extremely useful to see the differences between the support plans both in terms of the support perks and in the costs associated with each.

> **NOTE** For specific comparisons based on pricing, along with some pricing examples for specific situations, you can check out AWS Support Plan Pricing at https://aws.amazon.com/premiumsupport/pricing/.

CONSIDER THIS . . .

Let's imagine that you are an IT director at a medium-sized startup from the last section. Your organization has tested numerous AWS features and is committed to running its IT infrastructure on the AWS Cloud. Now, you need to evaluate the different types of support plans to find one that fits your company's needs and its operational budgets.

Using some of the tools we learned about in section 6.1, you've come to the conclusion that you're likely going to be spending $15,000 a month on AWS. Since your IT infrastructure is hosted on the AWS Cloud, it's considered production workloads, and it can't go down or become impaired for too long without risking serious business consequences.

While you obviously want the best-quality support, you're also cognizant of the realities of running on operational budgets and want to make sure you're being budget-conscious. As a result, you're willing to forego some bells and whistles as long as you are getting support when you need it. Which AWS support plan should you go with?

OUR SOLUTION . . .

The best bang-for-the-buck for you to receive the most amount of resources and support for the least amount of money is likely the Business Support Plan. The monthly support plan fee for $15,000 per month of AWS charges is 10% of $10,000, or $1,000, plus 7% of $5,000, or $350, for a total of $1,350 per month. This is in addition to the $15,000 in usage charges, which would bring your total monthly AWS bill to $16,350.

Since you're willing to forego many of the fancier features, such as a group or dedicated TAM and architectural and scaling guidance, the Business Support Plan will probably fit your needs, giving you the ability to create unlimited technical support cases and 24/7 access to AWS Cloud Support Engineers. The support response times are <4 hours for production system impaired and <1 hour for production system down, which is much better than the <12 hours for system impaired provided by the Developer Support Plan.

For quicker turnaround for support, you could consider the Enterprise On-Ramp Support Plan, but the monthly support fees associated would be $5,500 per month. This, in addition to the $15,000 usage bill, means that your organization would be paying over $20,500 per month in AWS bills.

For some organizations, that roughly $4,000 difference each month may be huge. For others, the quality and efficiency of the support they will receive, along with the proactive architectural support, may be worth it. Ultimately, it's up to your organization and your priorities.

THE "TOO LONG; DIDN'T READ" OF AWS SUPPORT PLANS

While there are definitely quite a lot of numbers and details you want to be aware of when comparing and contrasting the different support plans for potential use (or for exam questions), it is helpful to remember the "too long; didn't read" details of each support plan succinctly summarized here:

- *Basic Support Plan (free)*—For those testing out or experimenting with AWS
- *Developer Support Plan ($29/month and up)*—For those testing out or experimenting with AWS
- *Business Support Plan ($100/month and up)*—Minimum recommendation for those with production workloads in AWS (this is probably most likely scenario for most organizations and test questions)
- *Enterprise On-Ramp Support Plan ($5,500/month and up)*—For those with production-and/or business-critical workloads in AWS
- *Enterprise Support Plan ($15,000/month and up)*—For those with business- and/or mission-critical workloads in AWS

6.2.7 *Section quiz*

Robin has recently uploaded her startup's web application on the AWS Cloud and is getting ready to do a big public launch hopefully to begin having paying customers utilize her app. She is bootstrapping her startup and is not yet ready to commit to a hefty support plan bill every month but would like to make sure she has access to support via various channels and be confident that she can receive emergency support when her application goes down. Which support plan is the most appropriate for her startup?

  a The Basic Support Plan
  b The Developer Support Plan
  c The Business Support Plan
  d The Enterprise On-Ramp Support Plan
  e The Enterprise Support Plan

Summary

- The fundamental drivers of cost with AWS are compute, storage, and outbound data transfer charges.
- AWS's pricing models are pay as you go (on-demand), save when you commit (reserved instances), utilize leftover capacity (spot instances), and pay less by using-more.
- The AWS Free Tier offers over 100 AWS products to try out at no cost within three types of offerings: free trial, 12 months free, and always free.
- AWS Billing Dashboard is the default page of the AWS Billing Console and provides a general view of your AWS spending and usage.
- Consolidated billing allows organizations to receive one bill for all AWS accounts within the organization for easier accounting and potential volume discounts.
- There are many billing- and budgeting-related tools and calculators available to help you manage your AWS Cloud bills. Some we learned about were the AWS Pricing Calculator, the AWS Simple Monthly Calculator, the Migration Evaluator, AWS Budgets, the AWS Cost Explorer, the AWS Cost and Usage Report, and Amazon QuickSight.
- AWS offers many support plans for different needs and budgets. They are the Basic Support Plan, the Developer Support Plan, the Business Support Plan, the Enterprise On-Ramp Support Plan, and the Enterprise Support Plan.

Chapter quiz answers

- 6.1.6: c. You can set up a super-admin management account to manage all linked accounts and their resources.
  - *Answer*—AWS's consolidated billing feature allows you to receive one bill for all linked accounts within an organization, which includes combined

monthly charges, and the organization may be eligible for volume discounts. However, the management account is strictly for billing and accounting purposes, so it cannot provision resources or work as a super-admin account for all linked AWS accounts.

- 6.2.7: c. The Business Support Plan
  - *Answer*—The Business Support Plan starts at a rather affordable $100 per month and scales up with use. It provides <1 hour support response time for production system down, as well as 24/7 access to Cloud Support Engineers via phone, email, and chat. For Robin, these are important features, so rather than the Basic Support Plan or the Developer Support, the Business Support Plan is probably the most appropriate. The Enterprise On-Ramp and Enterprise Support Plans come with hefty price tags, which are likely not reasonable for a bootstrapped startup.

AWS Certified Cloud Practitioner exam (CLF-C01)

This chapter covers

- Diving into the AWS Certified Cloud Practitioner exam (CLF-C01)
- Reviewing the four domains of the CLF-C01 exam
- Interacting with study aids for the AWS Certified Cloud Practitioner exam

In the previous six chapters of this book, we've learned quite a large amount of information that helps us begin to construct a bird's-eye view of AWS and the value proposition of cloud computing in general. We began in chapter 1 by learning about the fundamentals of cloud computing and its value proposition, and we became familiar with AWS. In chapter 2, we learned about cloud concepts, and in chapter 3, we delved deeper into hosting IT infrastructure in AWS. Chapter 4 was a long one, in which we dipped our toes into dozens of core AWS services, and in chapter 5, we learned about security and compliance concepts as well as core security services. In chapter 6, we were introduced to AWS's billing and pricing concepts, tools, and the AWS support plan options.

In this final chapter of this book, we bring everything together to help you prepare for the AWS Certified Cloud Practitioner exam, which is AWS's only foundational-level exam as of 2022. We will learn about the AWS Certified Cloud Practitioner exam and the four domains that make up the exam and then move on to study aids to help you prepare. Let's get started!

7.1   Introducing the AWS Certified Cloud Practitioner exam

The AWS Certified Cloud Practitioner exam (CLF-C01) is a foundational-level certification exam offered by AWS to validate cloud fluency and—you guessed it—foundational AWS knowledge. Conveniently, that's exactly what we've been learning over the past six chapters, which means that, regardless of whether you picked up this book with the intention of studying for the AWS Certified Cloud Practitioner exam or not, you're actually pretty far along in your learning journey if you do decide to take it. Snazzy!

7.1.1   Why should I take the certification exam?

You may be wondering if there are really any benefits to taking the certification exam if you are not looking to become a cloud engineer or pursuing a career in another heavily technical cloud field. I think whether you take the certification exam or not is a personal decision, but there are real potential benefits to you and your career.

In the most immediate sense, if you pass an AWS certification exam, you receive a digital certificate. You can put it in your resume, and you can publish it on your LinkedIn profile so recruiters and potential employers can immediately recognize that you have passed this exam and have foundational AWS Cloud knowledge. Some employers will not only compensate for your exam study resources and the certification exam cost but may also consider bonuses or raises for achieving certain certifications. Some organizations are trying to get a particular number of their employees certified to reach certain standards or accreditations, so it's worth asking—there may be incentives for you to get certified.

I have heard of many people who work "around" the cloud (such as sales, accounting, or web designing) who have gained a huge sense of satisfaction and accomplishment when they validate their new AWS knowledge with a certification badge. The reasons to take the certification are many, and wanting to become a solutions architect or a cloud engineer isn't the only reason.

On a more social side, if you are into merch or attending AWS-hosted events, certified individuals are eligible to purchase special certified merchandise and are granted exclusive access to AWS Certification Lounges at AWS-hosted events. There are generally fewer people in the lounges, and they are often stocked with swag, coffee, and food, so it's a great way to network with fellow certified folks or meet up with people for a quick coffee break during a busy event!

7.1.2   *Official exam prep resources*

Before taking this exam, AWS recommends that you have specific hands-on experience that covers the exam content. However, the exam itself is purely knowledge-based, and there are no hands-on activities. While there are tons of third-party exam prep resources (like my own "Introduction to AWS for Non-Engineers" video courses hosted by LinkedIn Learning), AWS itself provides resources to supplement your learning, such as customized learning paths, digital and instructor-led trainings, exam readiness courses, white papers, AWS Free Tier, official practice questions, and blog articles. Check out this list of free official exam prep resources:

- AWS certification (https://aws.amazon.com/certification/)
- AWS Certified Cloud Practitioner official exam guide (http://mng.bz/neNe) (you can download the official exam guide, sample questions, and official practice question sets for free here)
- AWS Cloud Practitioner digital training (http://mng.bz/vX61)
- Exam readiness webinars (https://aws.amazon.com/training/events/)
- On-demand training on Twitch (http://mng.bz/494D)
- Introduction to AWS via AWS white papers (http://mng.bz/QnvR)

7.1.3   *Finding AWS support*

In many of the domains of this certification exam, AWS wants the candidate to identify resources for security and technology support. For this, AWS is generally asking you to acknowledge that you understand there are different options available to find solutions when you run into issues or get stuck, such as the following:

- Support forums
- Documentation (best practices, white papers, the AWS Knowledge Center, blogs)
- Support received through premium support plans
- Technical Account Managers and the Concierge Support Team (enterprise-level support plan customers only)
- AWS partners including vendors and system integrators
- Training and certification

7.1.4   *Target candidate description*

AWS has identified a target candidate for taking the AWS Certified Cloud Practitioner exam. However, the description is just a recommendation, and as long as you have the conceptual knowledge peppered throughout this book, you are well on your way. According to AWS, a target candidate should

- Have six months or equivalent active engagement with the AWS Cloud
- Have exposure to AWS Cloud design, implementation, and/or operations

- Demonstrate understanding of well-designed AWS Cloud solutions and architecture
- Have an understanding of AWS Cloud Concepts, core AWS services, and economics of the AWS Cloud
- Be knowledgeable about security and compliance within the AWS Cloud

Just as much as it describes what a candidate *should* know, AWS is also clear about what a candidate *doesn't* need to know and is not expected to perform for the certification exam. To me, this list seems almost as important as what you need to know, since it takes a lot of pressure off your mind. To successfully take and pass this certification exam, you *don't* need to know

- Coding
- Designing, troubleshooting, migrating, or implementing cloud architecture
- Load and performance testing
- Business applications/services (like Amazon Alexa, Amazon Chime, Amazon WorkMail)

7.1.5 *Exam quick facts*

We will spend the whole chapter going over the contents of the certification exam. However, first let me introduce you to a few exam quick facts to provide general information about the logistics of the exam.

- Successfully obtaining this certification helps organizations identify talents with cloud fluency and foundational AWS knowledge.
- There are four domains to the certification (we discuss them in more detail in the next section): Cloud Concepts, Security and Compliance, Technology, and Billing and Pricing
- The exam is a combination of 65 multiple choice (selecting one response out of multiple) and multiple response (selecting multiple responses) questions.
- The exam is 90 minutes long and costs $100. If you don't live in the United States, you can find out how much it costs in other countries here: http://mng .bz/XaZ1.
- You can take the exam at a testing center or as an online proctored exam.
- The exam is offered in English, French, German, Indonesian, Italian, Japanese, Korean, Portuguese (Brazil), Simplified Chinese, and Spanish (Latin America).
- A 30-minute exam extension is available for nonnative English speakers when taking the exam in English (accommodation "ESL +30").
- You can schedule the exam, download the official exam guide and sample questions, and find official AWS resources for preparing for the exam here: http://mng.bz/BZxw.

NOTE   Ready to go check out AWS's training and certification portal and perhaps even sign up for the exam? You can schedule and manage exams, view your certification history, take practice exams and free online courses, and more at AWS Training and Certification located at https://www.aws.training/Certification.

7.2   The four domains

As mentioned earlier, there are four domains in the AWS Certified Cloud Practitioner exam, with a different percentage of the exam assigned to each domain. The quick breakdown of the exam domains and their corresponding percentages are listed in table 7.1.

Table 7.1   **AWS Certified Cloud Practitioner exam domains**

Domain	% of Exam
Domain 1: Cloud Concepts	26
Domain 2: Security and Compliance	25
Domain 3: Technology	33
Domain 4: Billing and Pricing	16

Just because a smaller percentage of the exam content is devoted to one domain than another (such as Domain 4: Billing and Pricing with 16% compared to Domain 3: Technology with 33%), it does not mean that AWS considers any of these domains any more or less important than another. It's important to make sure you sit down for the exam with a well-rounded understanding of each domain and with the knowledge that there are more questions devoted to certain domains than others.

Take a look at figure 7.1 to review where we learned about each domain throughout this book. Isn't it pretty cool that while we seemed to be learning about cloud topics and concepts, we were actually working up to preparing for the AWS Certified Cloud Practitioner exam?

Before we go any further, I highly recommend that you download a PDF called the "AWS Certified Cloud Practitioner Exam Guide," available at http://mng.bz/BZxw. This official PDF is updated as the exam is updated and provides the most comprehensive (and straight from the source) content summary for the exam. We've spent the whole book learning the content we need to know for the four domains, so let's spend some time consolidating the information to see how we can best prepare for the exam.

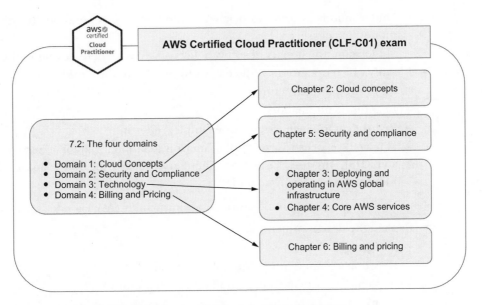

Figure 7.1 Where we learned about each domain in this book thus far

7.2.1 *Domain 1: Cloud Concepts*

The first domain for review is Domain 1: Cloud Concepts. This domain was covered in great detail in chapter 2 of this book.

I am directly citing the official AWS Certified Cloud Practitioner exam guide (version 2.1: http://mng.bz/lRad) on the breakdown of Domain 1: Cloud Concepts. There are some quick notes added to some of the bullet points to help jog your memory or links that help you quickly identify relevant resources.

After this next section, we head right into reviewing information we learned in the previous chapters that is relevant for this domain. Let's get started!

BREAKING DOWN DOMAIN 1: CLOUD CONCEPTS

Define the AWS Cloud and its value proposition (AWS Guide: 1.1):

- Define the benefits of the AWS Cloud including:
  - Security, reliability, high availability, elasticity, agility, pay-as-you go pricing, scalability, global reach, and economy of scale
- Explain how the AWS Cloud allows users to focus on business value:
  - Shifting technical resources to revenue-generating activities as opposed to managing infrastructure

Identify aspects of AWS Cloud economics (AWS Guide: 1.2):

- Define items that would be part of a Total Cost of Ownership proposal:
  - Understand the role of operational expenses (OpEx)
  - Understand the role of capital expenses (CapEx)

 – Understand labor costs associated with on-premises operations (think: time, money, expertise, etc.)
 – Understand the impact of software licensing costs when moving to the cloud
- Identify which operations reduce costs by moving to the cloud:
 – Right-sized infrastructure
 – Benefits of automation
 – Reduce compliance scope (for example, reporting)
 – Managed services (for example, Amazon Relational Database Service [Amazon RDS], Amazon Elastic Container Service [Amazon ECS], Amazon Elastic Kubernetes Service, DynamoDB)

Explain the different cloud architecture design principles (AWS Guide: 1.3):

- Explain the design principles:
 – Design for failure
 – Decouple components versus monolithic architecture
 – Implement elasticity in the cloud versus on-premises
 – Think parallel

Talking points for defining the AWS Cloud and its value proposition and identifying aspects of AWS Cloud economics come directly from the first cloud concepts we learned about, which introduced us to the six advantages of cloud computing. Let's quickly jog our memory. They are: trade capital expense for variable expense, benefit from massive economies of scale, stop guessing capacity, increase speed and agility, stop spending money running and maintaining data centers, and go global in minutes.

AWS wants you to be able to explain the different cloud architecture design principles that can be derived from the six pillars of a Well-Architected Framework (operational excellence, security, reliability, performance efficiency, cost optimization, and sustainability). Drawing blanks? Don't worry—we review these concepts again in the upcoming section.

While AWS uses words like *explain* and *describe*, you won't be asked to actively explain or describe anything, as it's a multiple choice/multiple answers exam. As long as you are able to identify the correct answer(s) from a list of potential solutions, you are good to go!

REVIEWING FOR DOMAIN 1: CLOUD CONCEPTS

In chapter 2, we learned about the value propositions of cloud computing, economics of cloud computing, and different design principles. These important ideas were summarized in few snappy cloud concepts.

Six advantages of cloud computing (section 2.2):

- *Trade capital expenses for variable expenses*—You only pay when and for what you consume (think: water/electricity bills).
- *Benefit from massive economies of scale*—Cloud computing platforms buy resource capacities in bulk to help you save money per-unit (think: Costco).

- *Stop guessing capacity*—Access as much (or as little) capacity as you need with flexible scaling.
- *Increase speed and agility*—Resources can be deployed or managed in minutes.
- *Stop spending money running and maintaining data centers*—No more physical infrastructures to set up and maintain (saves money, time, and labor).
- *Go global in minutes*—Deploy applications in multiple regions around the world with just a few clicks.

Three types of cloud computing models (section 2.3):

- *Software as a Service (SaaS)*—The complete product is managed by the service provider (for example, Gmail, Facebook).
- *Platform as a Service (PaaS)*—Deploy and manage applications without worrying about hardware infrastructure (like AWS Elastic Beanstalk, AWS Lambda, operating systems).
- *Infrastructure as a Service (IaaS)*—Physical/virtual IT infrastructure (such as data centers, physical buildings, servers, cloud computing platforms like AWS).

Three types of cloud computing deployments (section 2.4):

- *Cloud*—Whole infrastructure deployed on the cloud
- *Hybrid*—Mix of cloud and on-premises infrastructure
- *On-premises*—Infrastructure managed in your own data center

Six pillars of the Well-Architected Framework (section 2.5):

- *Operational excellence*—Daily system operations, monitoring, and improvements
- *Security*—Protecting information and systems
- *Reliability*—Ability to prevent and quickly recover from operational failures
- *Performance efficiency*—Using computing resources efficiently
- *Cost optimization*—Avoiding unnecessary costs
- *Sustainability*—Minimizing environmental impacts of cloud workloads

7.2.2 Domain 2: Security and Compliance

The second domain we are going to review is Domain 2: Security and Compliance. You may recall that there was a whole chapter in this book with the same title.

I am directly citing the official AWS Certified Cloud Practitioner exam guide (version 2.1: http://mng.bz/1Rad) on the breakdown of Domain 2: Security and Compliance. There are some quick notes added to some of the bullet points to help jog your memory or links that help you quickly identify relevant resources.

After this next section, we head right into reviewing information we learned in the previous chapters that is relevant for this domain. Let's keep going!

BREAKING DOWN DOMAIN 2: SECURITY AND COMPLIANCE

Define the AWS shared responsibility model (AWS Guide: 2.1):

- Recognize the elements of the shared responsibility model (who is responsible for security *of* the cloud vs security *in* the cloud).
- Describe the customer's responsibly on AWS:
  - Describe how the customer's responsibilities may shift depending on the service used (for example with Amazon RDS, Amazon Lambda, or Amazon Elastic Compute Cloud [EC2]).
  - Describe AWS responsibilities.

Define AWS Cloud security and compliance concepts (AWS Guide: 2.2):

- Identify where to find AWS compliance information:
  - Know locations of lists of recognized available compliance controls (for example, HIPAA, System and Organization Controls): https://aws.amazon .com/compliance/programs/.
  - Recognize that compliance requirements vary among AWS services.
- At a high level, describe how customers achieve compliance on AWS:
  - Identify different encryption options on AWS (for example, in transit, at rest).
- Describe who enables encryption on AWS for a given service.
- Recognize there are services that aid in auditing and reporting:
  - Recognize that logs exist for auditing and monitoring (do not have to understand the logs).
  - Define Amazon CloudWatch, AWS Config, and AWS CloudTrail.
- Explain the concept of least privileged access (only give as much access as necessary to complete the job).

Identify AWS access management capabilities (AWS Guide: 2.3):

- Understand the purpose of user and identity management (access to infrastructure and resources shouldn't be a free-for-all):
  - Access keys and password policies (rotation, complexity)
  - Multifactor authentication (MFA; secondary means of verifying identity)
  - AWS Identity and Access Management (AWS IAM; manage who can access what): groups/users, roles, policies (managed policies compared to custom policies (http://mng.bz/AVxe)
  - Tasks that require use of root accounts (we discuss these in detail in next section)
  - Protection of root accounts (don't use them unless absolutely necessary!)

Identify resources for security support (AWS Guide: 2.4):

- Recognize there are different network security capabilities:
  - Native AWS services (for example, security groups, network access control lists, AWS Web Application Firewall [WAF])
  - Third-party security products from the AWS Marketplace

- Recognize there is documentation and where to find it (for example, best practices, white papers, official documents):
  - AWS Knowledge Center, Security Center, security forum, and security blogs
  - Partner systems integrators (companies that aid in integrating different systems to create customized IT solutions)
- Know that security checks are a component of the AWS Trusted Advisor.

REVIEWING FOR DOMAIN 2: SECURITY AND COMPLIANCE

Going in order of the book is for squares! We are now looking into Domain 2: Security and Compliance, which we learned about in chapter 5. Some of the services we referred to in this book as *management tools* also come into play in this domain, and we learned about them in chapter 4.

Security and compliance concepts (section 5.1):

- *Shared responsibility model*—Responsibility for keeping your cloud IT infrastructure secure is a shared responsibility between the service provider (AWS) and the customer (you).
  - *Encryption*—Data should be protected *at rest* (while it's stored somewhere) and *in transit* (while it's moving from one place to another).
- *Security pillar of the Well-Architected Framework*—Best practices for protecting information and systems in the cloud.
  - Security in the cloud is composed of five areas: identity and access management (IAM), detective controls, infrastructure protection, data protection, incident response.
  - Multifactor authentication (MFA) adds an extra layer of security by enabling a *second factor* to verify user identity.
- *Principle of least privilege*—Every user/program should only be able to access information and resources necessary to complete their tasks successfully.

Security services and features (section 5.2):

- *AWS Identity and Access Management (IAM)*—Provides you with fine-grained permissions to secure AWS services and resources by defining *who* (workforce users, workloads) *can access* (permissions with IAM policies) *what* (resources), as shown in figure 7.2.

AWS identity and access management (IAM)

Who   can access   What

Figure 7.2   AWS Identity and Access Management helps you define who can access what.

- *Root account*—Account that has complete access to everything in your AWS account including all services and resources (think: God-tier account!); tasks that require use of the root account are as follows:
  - Change account settings (i.e., account name, email address, root user password, root access keys)
  - Restore IAM user permissions
  - Activate IAM access to Billing and Cost Management Console
  - View certain tax invoices
  - Close AWS account
  - Change or cancel AWS support plan
  - Register as seller in the Reserved Instance Marketplace
  - Configure MFA delete for Amazon Simple Cloud Storage (Amazon S3) bucket
  - Edit/delete Amazon S3 bucket policy that includes invalid Amazon Virtual Private Cloud (VPC) ID/Amazon VPC endpoint ID
  - Sign up for GovCloud (cloud platform for governments)
- *IAM policies*—Help you manage access to AWS resources and define an identity or resource's permissions when associated; there are six policy types:
  - Identity-based policies
  - Resource-based policies
  - Permissions boundaries
  - Organizations SCPs
  - Access control lists (ACLs)
  - Session policies
- *AWS Trusted Advisor*—AWS Trusted Advisor's security checks can help your organization's cloud IT infrastructure get as closely aligned with AWS's recommended best practices as possible to keep it secured.
- *AWS Web Application Firewall (AWS WAF)*—Firewall for web applications (another case of "exactly what the name says").
- *AWS Shield*—Distributed denial-of-service (DDoS) protection.
- *Amazon Inspector*—Automated security assessment for Amazon EC2 and Amazon Elastic Container Registry.
- *Amazon GuardDuty*—"Guards" your infrastructure from malicious activity.

Compliance services (section 4.5; we referred to them as management tools):

- *AWS CloudTrail*—Tracks "trails" of action (audit logs)
- *Amazon CloudWatch*—"Watches" (monitors) AWS
- *AWS Config*—Monitors service config(urations)

7.2.3 Domain 3: Technology

We are now moving on to the third domain, which covers technology. The Technology Domain encompasses both core AWS services and AWS's global infrastructure.

I am directly citing the official AWS Certified Cloud Practitioner exam guide (version 2.1: http://mng.bz/lRad) on the breakdown of Domain 3: Technology. There are some quick notes added to some of the bullet points to help jog your memory or links that help you quickly identify relevant resources.

After this next section, we review information we learned in the previous chapters that is relevant for this domain. We're almost through!

BREAKING DOWN DOMAIN 3: TECHNOLOGY

Define methods of deploying and operating in the AWS Cloud (AWS Guide: 3.1):

- Identify at a high level different ways of provisioning and operating in the AWS cloud:
  - Programmatic access, APIs, software development kids (SDKs), AWS Management Console, AWS Command Line Interface (CLI), Infrastructure as Code (IaC)
- Identify different types of cloud deployment models:
  - All in with cloud/cloud native
  - Hybrid
  - On-premises
- Identify connectivity options (ways for you/your infrastructure to communicate with AWS):
  - Virtual private network (VPN)
  - AWS Direct Connect
  - Public internet

Define the AWS global infrastructure (AWS Guide: 3.2):

- Describe the relationships between Regions, Availability Zones (AZs), and Edge Locations:
  - Regions have two or more AZs.
- Describe how to achieve high availability through the use of multiple AZs:
  - Recall that high availability is achieved by using multiple AZs.
  - Recognize that AZs do not share single points of failure.
- Describe when to consider the use of multiple AWS Regions:
  - Disaster recovery/business continuity
  - Low latency for end-users
  - Data sovereignty
- Describe at a high level the benefits of Edge Locations (caches data closest to your end user for faster loading time):
  - Amazon CloudFront
  - AWS Global Accelerator

Identify the core AWS services (AWS Guide: 3.3):

- Describe the categories of services on AWS (compute, storage, network, database).
- Identify AWS compute services:
  - Recognize there are different compute families.
  - Recognize the different services that provide compute (for example, AWS Lambda compared to Amazon ECS or Amazon EC2, etc.).
  - Recognize that elasticity is achieved through auto scaling.
  - Identify the purpose of load balancers.
- Identify different AWS storage services:
  - Describe Amazon S3, Amazon Elastic Block Store (Amazon EBS), Amazon S3 Glacier, AWS Snowball, Amazon Elastic File System (Amazon EFS), AWS Storage Gateway.
- Identify AWS networking services:
  - Identify VPC, VPN, AWS Direct Connect.
  - Identify security groups.
  - Identify the purpose of Amazon Route 53.
- Identify different AWS database services:
  - Install databases on Amazon EC2 compared to AWS managed databases (installing databases on Amazon EC2 would require you to spin up a virtual machine and then install and manage a database, whereas utilizing AWS managed databases cuts out the setting up/maintaining of virtual machines and the installation and management of a database, allowing you to interact directly with a database without the administrative overhead).
  - Identify Amazon RDS, Amazon DynamoDB, and Amazon Redshift.

Identify resources for technology support (AWS Guide: 3.4):

- Recognize there is documentation (best practices, white papers, AWS Knowledge Center, forums, blogs).
- Identify the various levels and scope of AWS support:
  - AWS abuse
  - AWS support cases
  - Premium support
  - Technical Account Managers
- Recognize there is a partner network (AWS Marketplace, third-party) including independent software vendors and system integrators.
- Identify sources of AWS technical assistance and knowledge including professional services, solution architects, training and certification, and the Amazon Partner Network.
- Identify the benefits of using AWS Trusted Advisor.

REVIEWING FOR DOMAIN 3: TECHNOLOGY

This domain is focused on the AWS Infrastructure, how you deploy and interact with AWS, and the core AWS services. Most of the content you need to review for Domain 3: Technology is nestled in chapters 3 and 4 of this book. However, there are few pieces, like the cloud deployment models, that reside in chapter 2. Given that this domain makes up 33% of the exam, you can expect quite a few questions on these topics.

Interacting with AWS (section 3.2):

- Programmatic access
- Graphical access
- Application programming interface (API)
- AWS software development kits (SDKs)
- AWS Management Console
- AWS Command Line Interface (CLI)
- Infrastructure as Code (IaC)

Cloud deployment models (section 2.4):

- *Cloud/cloud native*—Whole infrastructure deployed on the cloud
- *Hybrid*—Mix of cloud and on-premises infrastructure
- *On-premises*—Infrastructure managed in your own data center

Connecting to AWS (section 3.2.3):

- Virtual private network (VPN)
- AWS Direct Connect
- Public internet

AWS global infrastructure (section 3.3):

- *Regions*—Made up of two or more Availability Zones
- *Availability Zones (AZs)*—Discrete data centers
- *Edge Locations*—Physical data centers Amazon CloudFront uses to cache copies of data closest to end users
- *Amazon CloudFront*—Helps websites load faster by utilizing Edge Locations to cache data
- *AWS Global Accelerator*—Directs traffic over AWS global network; "accelerates" content delivery

Compute services (section 4.1):

- *Amazon Elastic Compute Cloud (Amazon EC2)*—Virtual server
- *AWS Elastic Beanstalk*—Automatically "grows" your app to meet demands like Jack's beanstalk
- *Elastic Load Balancing*—Balances incoming traffic loads
- *AWS Lambda*—Runs serverless code
- *Amazon Elastic Container Service (Amazon ECS)*—Container orchestration service

Storage services (section 4.2):

- *Amazon Simple Storage Service (Amazon S3)*—Object storage
- *Amazon S3 Glacier*—Long-term/archival object storage (data is "frozen" like a glacier; cheaper)
- *Amazon Elastic Block Store (Amazon EBS)*—Block storage; virtual drive
- *AWS Snowball*—Transfers huge amounts of data to AWS (physical device).
- *AWS Storage Gateway*—Gateway to connect on-premises with the cloud
- *Amazon Elastic File System (Amazon EFS)*—"Elastic" file system that scales up/down on demand

Networking and content delivery services (section 4.4):

- *Amazon Virtual Private Cloud (Amazon VPC)*—Virtual network (your corner of the cloud)
- *AWS Direct Connect*—Directly connects a local network to AWS
- *Amazon Virtual Private Network (Amazon VPN)*—Virtual private network (yup)
- *Amazon CloudFront*—Speedy websites (imagine: front of race); uses Edge Locations
- *AWS Global Accelerator*—Directs traffic over AWS global network; accelerates content delivery
- *Amazon Route 53*—Routes domains to services/IP addresses; cloud DNS (think: phonebook)

Database services (section 4.3):

- *Amazon Relational Database Service (Amazon RDS)*—Relational database
- *Amazon Aurora*—Relational database (runs on Amazon RDS)
- *Amazon DynamoDB*—Nonrelational database (NoSQL)
- *Amazon Redshift*—Data warehouse (*lots* of data and data analysis)

Management tools (section 4.5):

- *AWS CloudFormation*—Templates to form cloud infrastructure
- *AWS CloudTrail*—Tracks "trails" of action (audit logs)
- *Amazon CloudWatch*—"Watches" (monitors) AWS
- *AWS Config*—Monitors service config(urations)
- *AWS Trusted Advisor*—Checks to optimize infrastructure (performance, cost optimization, security, fault tolerance)

7.2.4   *Domain 4: Billing and Pricing*

We are wrapping up on the domains with the tedious but still necessary money talk with the Billing and Pricing Domain of the AWS Certified Cloud Practitioner exam. I am directly citing the official AWS Certified Cloud Practitioner exam guide (version 2.1: http://mng.bz/lRad) on the breakdown of Domain 4: Billing and Pricing. There are some quick notes added to some of the bullet points to help jog your memory or links that help you quickly identify relevant resources.

After this next section, we review information we learned in the previous chapters that is relevant for this domain. Let's crank through the last domain!

BREAKING DOWN DOMAIN 4: BILLING AND PRICING

Compare and contrast the various pricing models for AWS (for example, On-Demand Instances, Reserved Instances, and Spot Instance pricing) (AWS Guide: 4.1):

- Identify scenarios/best fit for On-Demand Instance pricing ("regular priced" but flexible).
- Identify scenarios/best fit for Reserved Instance pricing (cheaper but requires a commitment):
  - Describe Reserved Instances flexibility
  - Describe Reserved Instances behavior in AWS organizations
- Identify scenarios/best fit for Spot Instance pricing (cheaper but not consistent; utilizing leftover capacity).

Recognize the various account structures in relation to AWS billing and pricing (AWS Guide: 4.2):

- Recognize that consolidated billing is a feature of AWS organizations (pay for multiple accounts' monthly AWS bills using one billing account).
- Identify how multiple accounts aid in allocating costs across departments (know who's using what).

Identify resources available for billing support (AWS Guide: 4.3):

- Identify ways to get billing support and information:
  - Cost Explorer, AWS Cost and Usage Report, Amazon QuickSight, third-party partners, and AWS Marketplace tools.
  - Open a billing support case.
  - The role of the Concierge Support Team for AWS enterprise support plan customers.
- Identify where to find pricing information on AWS services:
  - AWS Simple Monthly Calculator
  - AWS Services product pages
  - AWS pricing API
- Recognize that alarms/alerts exist (beep beep!).
- Identify how tags are used in cost allocation (Whose resource is it? What is it used for?).

REVIEWING FOR DOMAIN 4: BILLING AND PRICING

This domain deals with how billing for AWS Cloud usage works, as well as the different pricing models and methods. You need to have a good grasp of the AWS support plans and how they differ to choose which plan is best for a provided scenario. This knowledge helps you to choose an appropriate support plan for your projects or organization when the time comes. We also learned about quite a few tools and calculators so you can set up your organization for financial success by accurately predicting (and at times analyzing past) resource usage.

Chapter 6 was devoted to billing and pricing topics and tools. As you may recall, we learned about concepts like the AWS pricing models, consolidated billing, types of services offered for free via AWS Free Tier, different tools to visualize AWS's billing and pricing, and the AWS support plans available.

AWS pricing models (section 6.1.1):

- *On-demand pricing*—Pay as you go
- *Reserved Instances*—Save when you commit
- *Spot Instances*—Take advantage of unused AWS capacity
- *Pay less by using more*—Pay less per-unit by utilizing more resources

Billing account structures (section 6.1.4):

- *Consolidated billing*—Allows consolidated payments from multiple AWS accounts within an organization (linked accounts) by a single designated billing/accounting account (management account)

AWS Free Tier (section 6.1.2):

- Free trial
- 12 months free
- Always free

AWS support plans (section 6.2):

- *Basic Support Plan*—For testing out/experimenting with AWS (free)
- *Developer Support Plan*—For testing out/experimenting with AWS (starts at $29/month)
- *Business Support Plan*—Minimum recommendation for production workloads in AWS (starts at $100/month)
- *Enterprise On-Ramp Support Plan*—For production- and/or business-critical workloads in AWS (starts at $5,500/months)
- *Enterprise Support Plan*—For business- and/or mission-critical workloads in AWS (starts at $15,000/months)

Visualizing billing and pricing (section 6.1.5):

- *AWS Billing Dashboard (section 6.1.3)*—Provides a dashboard with general view of AWS spending and usage (part of AWS Billing Console).
- *AWS Pricing Calculator*—Enter estimated resource usage and receive a cost estimate for running infrastructure on AWS.
- *Cost Explorer*—Visualize/analyze AWS Cloud spend after the fact.

- *AWS Cost and Usage Report*—Create daily reports with comprehensive set of AWS cost and usage data to help identify cost drivers and usage optimizations.
- *AWS Simple Monthly Calculator*—Estimate monthly cost of various AWS services based on expected use-case scenarios.
- *Migration Evaluator*—Create data-driven business cases for planning/migrating IT infrastructure to AWS.
- *AWS Budgets*—Set custom budgets to track AWS resource usage and costs associated with infrastructure.
- *Amazon QuickSight*—Create customized dashboards to visualize all sorts of data including for AWS billing/cost-related information.

7.3   AWS Certified Cloud Practitioner exam study aids

When I was studying for the AWS Certified Cloud Practitioner exam, I spent quite a bit of time looking for flash-card–type content to help me do quick knowledge checks. Unfortunately at the time, I didn't find any, so I ended up having to come up with some myself. Today, there may be some resources available, but it never hurts to have more.

So here we are, with some exam study aids that I wish I had when I was studying for this exam. They include:

- Cloud concepts in a flash
- Core AWS services flashcards
- AWS support plans table

I hope these tools help you while you are studying, and while you're doing your last-minute knowledge checks before your exam. Good luck!

7.3.1   Cloud concepts in a flash

There are a few core concepts that you need to more or less memorize for the certification exam to quickly knock out questions related to them. I've listed them here for quick retrieval and last-minute pre-exam studying.

SIX ADVANTAGES OF CLOUD COMPUTING (SECTION 2.2)

- *Trade capital expense for variable expense*—You only pay when and for what you consume (think: water/electricity bills).
- *Benefit from massive economies of scale*—Cloud computing platforms buy resource capacities in bulk to help you save money per unit (think: Costco).
- *Stop guessing capacity*—Access as much (or as little) capacity as you need with flexible scaling.
- *Increase speed and agility*—Resources can be deployed or managed in minutes.
- *Stop spending money running and maintaining data centers*—No more physical infrastructures to set up and maintain (saves money, time, and labor).
- *Go global in minutes*—Deploy applications in multiple regions around the world with just a few clicks.

THREE TYPES OF CLOUD COMPUTING MODELS (SECTION 2.3)

As shown in figure 7.3, the level of control you have over the resources with each cloud computing model goes up as you go down the list, but some require more engineering expertise to configure and maintain.

Figure 7.3   The three types of cloud computing models that reflect the different technical needs and requirements are SaaS, PaaS, and IaaS.

- *Software as a Services (SaaS)*—Completely product-managed by a service provider (like Gmail, Facebook)
- *Platform as a Service (PaaS)*—Deploy and manage applications without worrying about hardware infrastructure (for example, AWS Elastic Beanstalk, AWS Lambda, operating systems)
- *Infrastructure as a Services (IaaS)*—Physical/virtual IT infrastructure (such as data centers, physical buildings, servers, cloud computing platforms like AWS)

THREE TYPES OF CLOUD COMPUTING DEPLOYMENTS (SECTION 2.4)

- Cloud/cloud native—Whole infrastructure deployed on the cloud
- Hybrid—Mix of cloud and on-premises infrastructure
- On-premises—Infrastructure managed in your own data center

SIX PILLARS OF THE WELL-ARCHITECTED FRAMEWORK (SECTION 2.5)

There are six pillars of AWS's Well-Architected Framework, as represented in figure 7.4:

- *Operational excellence*—Daily system operations, monitoring, and improvements
- *Security*—Protects information and systems
- *Reliability*—Ability to prevent and quickly recover from operational failures
- *Performance efficiency*—Using computing resources efficiently
- *Cost optimization*—Avoiding unnecessary costs
- *Sustainability*—Minimize environmental impacts of cloud workloads

Six pillars of AWS's Well-Architected Framework

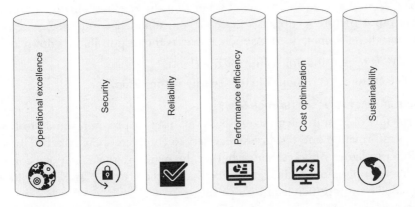

Figure 7.4 **The six pillars that make up AWS's Well-Architected Framework are operational excellence, security, reliability, performance efficiency, cost optimization, and sustainability.**

AWS GLOBAL INFRASTRUCTURE (SECTION 3.3)

As figure 7.5 shows, the AWS global infrastructure is made up of Regions. Regions are made up of two or more Availability Zones (AZs), which are logical data centers. Copies of cached data are stored at Edge Locations closest to end users to provide quicker download speeds.

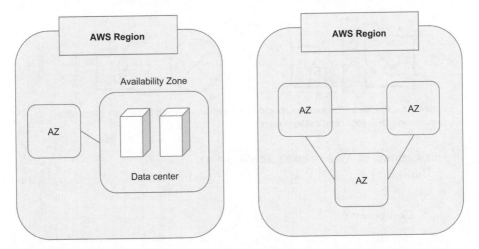

Figure 7.5 **AWS Regions are distinct physical locations around the world with two or more AZs, and AZs are logical data centers.**

- *Regions*—Made up of two or more AZs
- *Availability Zones (AZs)*—Discrete data centers
- *Edge Locations*—Physical data centers Amazon CloudFront uses to cache copies of data closest to end users

SHARED RESPONSIBILITY MODEL (SECTION 5.1.1)

The AWS shared responsibility model states that the responsibility for keeping your cloud IT infrastructure secured is a shared responsibility between the service provider (AWS) and the customer (you). As such, it breaks the responsibilities down as follows:

- AWS is responsible for security *of* the cloud.
- The customer is responsible for security *in* the cloud.

PRINCIPLE OF LEAST PRIVILEGE (SECTION 5.1.3)

The principle of least privilege states that every user or program should only be able to access information and resources necessary to complete their tasks or jobs successfully. Refer to figure 7.6 to evaluate whether the marketing manager of a company or the cafeteria operations manager should have access to the Marketing Resources folder based on this principle of least privilege.

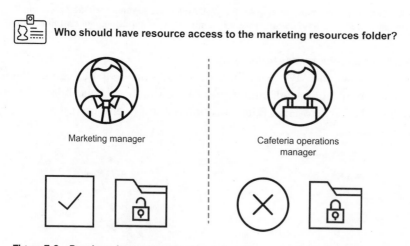

Figure 7.6   People and resources should only be given as much access as necessary to complete their jobs, and nothing more.

FUNDAMENTALS OF AWS PRICING (SECTION 6.1.1)

As shown in figure 7.7, there are three fundamental ways AWS charges for resource usage:

- Compute
- Storage
- Outbound data transfer

Compute   Storage   Outbound data
                                   transfer

Figure 7.7   The three fundamental ways you will be charged for utilizing AWS Cloud are compute, storage, and outbound data transfer.

AWS PRICING MODELS (SECTION 6.1.1)

- *On-demand pricing*—Pay as you go.
- *Reserved Instances*—Save when you commit.
- *Spot Instances*—Take advantage of unused AWS capacity.
- *Pay less by using more*—Pay less per unit by utilizing more resources.

AWS TRUSTED ADVISOR (SECTION 4.5.5)

AWS Trusted Advisor walks around your IT infrastructure with a checklist in hand, looking for ways to optimize your IT infrastructure. This auditing service offers recommendations using checks. AWS Trusted Advisor's checks are categorized as follows:

- Cost optimization
- Performance
- Security
- Fault tolerance
- Service quotas

The scope of checks available depends on the AWS support plan your organization is enrolled in:

- *AWS Basic and AWS Developer Support Plans*—Core security checks, all checks for service quotas
- *AWS Business and AWS Enterprise-level Support Plans*—All checks including cost optimization, security, fault tolerance, performance, and service quotas

7.3.2   Core AWS services flashcards

When I was studying for the AWS Certification exam, I had a very difficult time locating a list of services on the exam and a super-quick description that I could potentially make into flashcards to study. Having no success, I ended up creating one of my own, and it has been living on awsnewbies.com for a few years.

Now, I present to you an updated version with more services that were recently added to the AWS Certified Cloud Practitioner exam. I hope these flashcards help you to more efficiently do last-minute preparations for the exam.

COMPUTE SERVICES

- *Amazon Elastic Compute Cloud (Amazon EC2)*—Virtual server
- *AWS Elastic Beanstalk*—Automatically "grows" your app to meet demands like Jack's beanstalk
- *Elastic Load Balancing*—Balances incoming traffic loads
- *AWS Lambda*—Runs serverless code
- *Amazon Elastic Container Service (Amazon ECS)*—Container orchestration service (exactly what the name says)

STORAGE SERVICES

- *Amazon Simple Storage Service (Amazon S3)*—Object storage
- *Amazon Elastic Block Store (Amazon EBS)*—Block storage; virtual drive
- *AWS Snowball*—Transfers huge amounts of data to AWS (physical device)
- *AWS Storage Gateway*—Gateway to connect on-premises with the cloud
- *Amazon Elastic File System (Amazon EFS)*—"Elastic" file system that scales up/down on-demand

DATABASE SERVICES

- *Amazon Relational Database Service (Amazon RDS)*—Relational database
- *Amazon Aurora*—Relational database (runs on Amazon RDS)
- *Amazon DynamoDB*—Nonrelational database (NoSQL)
- *Amazon Redshift*—Data warehouse (*lots* of data and data analysis)

NETWORKING AND CONTENT DELIVERY SERVICES

- *Amazon Virtual Private Cloud (Amazon VPC)*—Virtual network (your "corner" of the Cloud)
- *AWS Direct Connect*—"Directly connects" local network to AWS
- *Amazon Virtual Private Network (Amazon VPN)*—Virtual private network (yup)
- *Amazon CloudFront*—Speedy websites (think: front of race); uses Edge Locations
- *AWS Global Accelerator*—Directs traffic over AWS global network; "accelerates" content delivery
- *Amazon Route 53*—Routes domains to services/IP services; cloud DNS

MANAGEMENT TOOLS

- *AWS CloudFormation*—Templates to "form" cloud infrastructure
- *AWS CloudTrail*—Tracks "trails" of action (audit logs)
- *Amazon CloudWatch*—"Watches" (monitors) AWS.
- *AWS Config*—Monitors service config(urations)
- *AWS Trusted Advisor*—Checks to optimize infrastructure (performance, cost optimization, security, fault tolerance)

SECURITY SERVICES

- *AWS Identity and Access Management (AWS IAM)*—Create accounts, provide access
- *AWS Web Application Firewall (AWS WAF)*—Firewall for web apps (another case of "exactly what the name says")
- *AWS Shield*—Distributed denial-of-service (DDoS) protection
- *Amazon Inspector*—Automated security assessment for Amazon EC2 and Amazon Elastic Container Registry
- *Amazon GuardDuty*—"Guards" your infrastructure from malicious activity

7.3.3   *AWS support plans*

Most of what you need to accomplish with the AWS support plans in terms of the AWS Certified Cloud Practitioner exam revolves around evaluating provided scenarios and deciding which support plan would be the most optimal for the given situation. There are five different AWS Support Plans that should ideally match your level of support need and budget. They are as follows (with more details in table 7.2):

- *Basic Support Plan*—For testing out/experimenting with AWS (free)
- *Developer Support Plan*—For testing out/experimenting with AWS (starts at $29/month)
- *Business Support Plan*—Minimum recommendation for production workloads in AWS (starts at $100/month)
- *Enterprise On-Ramp Support Plan*—For production and/or business critical workloads in AWS (starts at $5,500/month)
- *Enterprise Support Plan*—For business and/or mission critical workloads in AWS (starts at $15,000/month)

You can utilize sample exam questions on the official AWS website to get the gist of the types of questions AWS will ask, but in general, AWS will likely provide a scenario with the following information:

- Type and size of organization
- How much money the organization has—or doesn't have—to spend on support
- What kind of support the organization is looking for
- Whether the organization has production workload on AWS or not

Using the information provided, you need to make an educated guess on which support plan is the best match. While in theory, everyone would love to have the white-gloved support that the Enterprise Support Plan provides, but in reality, most organizations can't afford it. With the introduction of the Enterprise On-Ramp Support Plan, AWS now offers a more budget-friendly option (although it's still quite expensive). You'll need to make sure you know the pricing for each option to help make the decision, balancing the perks with the costs associated.

Table 7.2   AWS support plans

Basic Support Plan	Developer Support Plan	Business Support Plan
For testing out/experimenting with AWS (great for AWS Free Tier)	For testing out/experimenting with AWS	Minimum recommendation for those with production workloads in AWS
<ul><li>1:1 response for account and billing inquiries</li><li>Access to support forums, like AWS re:Post</li><li>Service health checks (remember AWS Trusted Advisor?)</li><li>Access to documentation, technical papers, best practice guides</li><li>Access to AWS Personal Health Dashboard</li></ul>	<ul><li>Everything in Basic Support Plan</li><li>Best practices guidance</li><li>Access to client-side diagnostic tools</li><li>Access to building-block architecture support that provide guidance on how to utilize the different AWS products, features, and services together effectively</li><li>Ability to have an unlimited number of support cases opened via one primary contact (your AWS account's root user)</li><li>Business hours email access to Cloud Support Associates</li><li>Support response times: <24 hours for general guidance, <12 hours for system impaired</li><li>Prioritized responses on AWS re:Post</li><li>Access to Support Automation Workflows with prefixes *AWSSupport*</li></ul>	<ul><li>Everything in Developer Support Plan</li><li>Access to use-case guidance that helps you map out what AWS products features, and services you should utilize to support your specific needs</li><li>Ability to utilize full set of checks with the AWS Trusted Advisor's Best Practice Checks</li><li>Access to the AWS Support API to interact with AWS Trusted Advisor and the Support Center</li><li>Interoperability and configuration troubleshooting for popular third-party software components on AWS and Amazon EC2 operating systems</li><li>Ability for unlimited number of AWS IAM users to open unlimited number of technical support cases</li><li>24/7 phone, email, and chat access to AWS Cloud Support Engineers</li><li>Support response times: <24 hours for general guidance, <12 hours for system impaired, <4 hours for production system impaired, and <1 hour for production system down</li><li>Access to Support Automation Workflows with prefixes *AWSSupport* and *AWSPremiumSupport*</li><li>Receive Infrastructure Event Management (additional fee)</li></ul>
<ul><li>Free</li></ul>	Greater of:<ul><li>$29 *or*</li><li>3% of your monthly AWS charges</li></ul>	Greater of:<ul><li>$100 *or*</li><li>10% of your monthly AWS charges for first $0~$10,000</li><li>7% of monthly AWS charges from $10,000~$80,000</li><li>5% of monthly AWS charges from $80,000~$250,000</li><li>3% of monthly AWS usage over $250,000</li></ul>

Table 7.2 AWS support plans *(continued)*

Enterprise On-Ramp Support Plan	Enterprise Support Plan
For those with production and/or business critical workloads in AWS	For those with business and/or mission critical workloads in AWS
■ Everything in Business Support Plan ■ Access to consultative application architecture guidance on how AWS services and resources fit together to meet your specific use case ■ Receive short-term engagement with AWS Support to receive architectural and scaling guidance for Infrastructure Event Management once a year ■ Have access to a pool of Technical Account Managers to support your specific use cases and applications, provide proactive guidance, and coordinate support through programs and AWS experts ■ Receive white-gloved case routing via the Concierge Support Team ■ Access to management business reviews ■ Support response times: <24 hours for general guidance, <12 hours for system impaired, <4 hours for production system impaired, <1 hour for production system down, <30 minutes for business-critical system down	■ Everything in Enterprise On-Ramp Support Plan ■ Receive Infrastructure Event Management ■ Access to proactive workshops, reviews, and deep dives for your organization ■ Assigned to a designated Technical Account Manager to proactively monitor and assist with optimization for your AWS Cloud environment, as well as coordinate access to AWS experts and relevant programs for your organization ■ Access to online self-paced labs for employee training ■ Support Response Times: <24 hours for general guidance, <12 hours for system impaired, <4 hours for production system impaired, <1 hour for production system down, <15 minutes for business/mission-critical system down
Greater of: ■ $5,500 *or* ■ 10% of your monthly AWS charges	Greater of: ■ $15,000 *or* ■ 10% of your monthly AWS charges for first $0~$150,000 ■ 7% of monthly AWS charges from $150,000~$500,000 ■ 5% of monthly AWS charges from $500,000~$1 million ■ 3% of monthly AWS charges over $1 million

Summary

- The AWS Certified Cloud Practitioner exam is a foundational-level exam offered by AWS Cloud to validate the candidate's cloud fluency and foundational AWS knowledge.
- There are four domains in the AWS Certified Cloud Practitioner exam: Cloud Concepts (26%), Security and Compliance (25%), Technology (33%), and Billing and Pricing (16%).
- The AWS Certified Cloud Practitioner exam is 65 questions (multiple choice/multiple response questions), 90 minutes long, and costs $100. You can take it at a testing center or as an online proctored exam.
- Cloud concepts that are important to understand for the AWS Certified Cloud Practitioner exam are the six advantages of cloud computing, types of cloud computing models, types of cloud computing deployments, and the six pillars of AWS's Well-Architected Framework.

- Security and compliance concepts that are important to understand for the AWS Certified Cloud Practitioner exam are the shared responsibility model, the security pillar of AWS's Well-Architected Framework, and the principle of least privilege.

- The five types of AWS support plans are the Basic Support Plan, Developer Support Plan, Business Support Plan, Enterprise On-Ramp Support Plan, and Enterprise Support Plan. You are charged for the support plans in addition to your monthly AWS resource usage bill.

- There are sets of core AWS services that you should be familiar with for the AWS Certified Cloud Practitioner exam. They are broadly categorized into compute services, storage services, database services, networking and content delivery services, management tools, and security services:
  - *Compute services*—Amazon Elastic Compute Cloud (Amazon EC2), AWS Elastic Beanstalk, Elastic Load Balancing, AWS Lambda, and Amazon Elastic Container Service (Amazon ECS)
  - *Storage services*—Amazon Simple Storage Service (Amazon S3), Amazon Elastic Block Store (Amazon EBS), AWS Snowball, AWS Storage Gateway, and Amazon Elastic File System (Amazon EFS)
  - *Database services*—Amazon Relational Database (Amazon RDS), Amazon Aurora, Amazon DynamoDB, and Amazon Redshift
  - *Networking and content delivery services*—Amazon Virtual Private Cloud (Amazon VPC), Amazon Direct Connect, Amazon Virtual Private Network (Amazon VPN), Amazon CloudFront, AWS Global Accelerator, and Amazon Route 53
  - *Management tools*—AWS CloudFormation, AWS CloudTrail, Amazon CloudWatch, AWS Config, and AWS Trusted Advisor
  - *Security services*—AWS Identity and Access Management (AWS IAM), AWS Web Application Firewall (AWS WAF), AWS Shield, Amazon Inspector, Amazon GuardDuty

- There are many places to seek support when you're stuck or have technical issues. Some of them are support forums, documentation, premium support plans, Technical Account Managers, and the Concierge Support Team (Enterprise-level support plans only), AWS Partners including vendors and system integrators, and training and certification resources.

- This may all be overwhelming (I know I was completely overwhelmed), but take a deep breath—you're going to do great! (And hey, if not this time, there's always a next time.)

index

RELATED MANNING TITLES

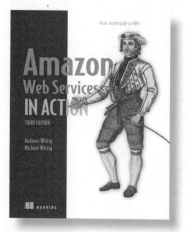

Amazon Web Services in Action
Third Edition
by Andreas Wittig and Michael Wittig

ISBN 9781633439160
500 pages *(estimated)*, $59.99
Spring 2023 *(estimated)*

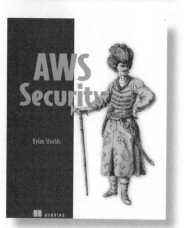

AWS Security
by Dylan Shields

ISBN 9781617297335
312 pages, $59.99
August 2022

For ordering information go to www.manning.com

RELATED MANNING TITLES

Serverless Architectures on AWS
Second Edition
by Peter Sbarski, Yan Cui, and Ajay Nair

ISBN 9781617295423
256 pages, $49.99
February 2022

AI as a Service
by Peter Elger and Eóin Shanaghy

ISBN 9781617296154
328 pages, $49.99
September 2020

For ordering information go to www.manning.com

A new online reading experience

liveBook, our online reading platform, adds a new dimension to your Manning books, with features that make reading, learning, and sharing easier than ever. A liveBook version of your book is included FREE with every Manning book.

This next generation book platform is more than an online reader. It's packed with unique features to upgrade and enhance your learning experience.

- Add your own notes and bookmarks
- One-click code copy
- Learn from other readers in the discussion forum
- Audio recordings and interactive exercises
- Read all your purchased Manning content in any browser, anytime, anywhere

As an added bonus, you can search every Manning book and video in liveBook—even ones you don't yet own. Open any liveBook, and you'll be able to browse the content and read anything you like.*

Find out more at www.manning.com/livebook-program.

Open reading is limited to 10 minutes per book daily